Some Voices
&
Pale Horse

'One of last year's most striking debuts in the Royal Court's Theatre Upstairs was Joe Penhall's *Some Voices*. His second Court play, *Pale Horse*, is as compelling and extraordinary as his first.' *Observer*

'**Some Voices** is a beautifully written piece focusing on Ray, a young schizophrenic trying to get back on the rails. . . It's dark material, but Penhall handles it with a light touch. He doesn't romanticise Ray, neither does he vilify his brother, and their relationship is riveting.' *Independent*

'**Pale Horse** is compelling and rivetingly well written. . . Charlie Strong has lost his wife; you gradually gather that he is a violent man. . . Soon there is more bloody violence, and Charlie, who is still in shock after his bereavement, gets increasingly out of control. You are gripped by the moody dialogue.' *Sunday Times*

Joe Penhall lives in London. His first play, *Wild Turkey*, was performed at the Old Red Lion as part of the 1993 London New Play Festival. *Some Voices* (1994, Royal Court Theatre Upstairs) won him a Thames Television Bursary and the John Whiting Award in 1995 and was shortlisted for the Lloyds Private Banking Playwright of the Year Award, the Verity Bargate Award and the British Writers Guild Best Fringe Play. *Pale Horse* (1995, Royal Court Theatre Upstairs) won the Thames Television Best Play Award. Joe is writer in residence at the Royal National Theatre.

Joe Penhall

Some Voices
&
Pale Horse

Methuen Drama

Methuen Drama Modern Plays

First published in Great Britain in 1996
by Methuen Drama

Some Voices first published in 1995 by Methuen Drama in *Frontline Intelligence 3*
copyright © 1995 by Joe Penhall

Pale Horse published in 1995 by Methuen Drama
copyright © 1995 by Joe Penhall

The author has asserted his moral rights

ISBN 0 413 70440 8

A CIP catalogue record for this book is available at the British Library

Typeset by Wilmaset Ltd, Wirral
Transferred to digital printing 2004

Caution

Contents

Some Voices

for absent friends

Some Voices was first performed at the Royal Court Theatre
Upstairs, London, in association with the Royal National
Theatre Studio on 15 September 1994. The cast was as follows:

Dave	Lloyd Hutchinson
Laura	Anna Livia Ryan
Ray	Lee Ross
Ives	Tom Watson
Pete	Ray Winstone

Directed by Ian Rickson
Designed by Rae Smith
Lighting by Jim Simmons
Sound by Paul Arditti
Music by Stephen Warbeck

Characters

Ray, *in his early twenties*
Laura, *Irish, the same age*
Pete, *Ray's brother, in his early thirties*
Dave, *Irish, the same age*
Ives, *around fifty*

The action takes place over a period of about six weeks in west
London.

Note
An oblique/stroke within a speech serves as the cue for the next
speaker to overlap with the first.

Act One

Scene One

Mental hospital. **Ray** *is standing by a window, a suitcase at his feet.* **Ives** *is nearby.*

Ray   You shat on my window sill again, didn't you, Ives?

Ives   No.

Ray   Yes you did. You were drunk again and you couldn't be bothered –

Ives   No.

Ray   Couldn't be bothered going to the toilet so you –

Ives   Bring me your shit!

Ray   So you went to the window and dropped a turd out of your window and it landed on my window/sill.

Ives   Bring me your shit!

Ray   You did. It's the only explanation. (*Sniffs.*) Jesus, it's disgusting.

Pause.

Ives   Are you a betting man?

Ray   Don't change the subject.

Ives   Like the horses, do you?

Ray   No I don't.

Ives   I used to like following around behind the horses and scooping up their shit.

Ray   Well, why don't you scoop/up your own?

Ives   It gave me something to do. Would you like to scoop up my shit?

Ray   No.

Ives   Because I would like somebody to scoop up my shit. I am tired of scooping up other people's shit. Somebody should scoop up mine. That's why I leave it there.

Ray   Where d'you get the booze from, Ives?

Ives   I ought to rub your nose in it.

Ray   *What?*

Ives   Then you'd learn.

Ray   But it's yours.

Ives *puts a hand on the back of* **Ray**'*s neck.*

Ray   Hey, Ives, Ives –

Ives   Do you know what they do to me?

Ray   What?

Ives   Everything. Worm balls in my mouth, fur balls in my mouth, tape-recordings. They play the tape-recorded voices then they make me eat them.

Ray   Who does?

Ives   The loonies. They think that I'm loony too. They think that just because they like it, I like it. But I never liked it. Not in my food for God's sake – it's weird.

Ray (*beat*)   You could complain.

Ives   I *am* complaining. I am complaining to you and you're not even listening!

Ives *lets go of* **Ray**. *Pause. They look at each other.*

Ray   I have to get going.

Ives   Where?

Ray   I'm going home. They're letting me out today.

Ives   No they're not.

Ray   They are, Ives.

Ives   They're just 'letting you out'. Just like that. Listen to me, you'll never survive out there. They know it, you know it. They been promising to let me out for years – years – and they haven't. Why? I don't know why.

Ray They don't want me any more, Ives. I'm not crazy enough.

Ives I think you're crazy.

Ray My time's up.

Ives You're damn right your time's up.

Ray My twenty-eight/days.

Ives You're fucking right your time is up.

Ray I'm/off.

Ives Everybody's time is up. You only have to look at things out there. A world which drives people bananas.

They look at each other. **Ray** *takes out a piece of paper from his pocket and scrawls on it. Hands it to* **Ives** *who reads it and stuffs it in his mouth.*

Ray This is my brother's address. When you get out, look me up.

Ives Twenty years I been here and never once has anyone offered to let me out. They made me eat shit. Not horse shit, real shit. I try to kill myself all the time and they stop me. They don't even care.

Ray I'm going now.

Ives They pretend to care – they profess to know how to be in the business of caring, which to me, sonny Jim, is no different to a butcher professing to know how to operate on the brain. I like it here. D'you understand? I love it! They won't/get rid of me.

Ray Ives –

Ives I belong here.

Ray I'll see you round.

Ives Probably yes probably birds of a feather and all that.

Ray What?

Ives Stick together.

Ray   Yeh.

Ives *clutches* **Ray**'s *arm to stop him leaving.*

Ives   You are marked, my friend. Do you understand me?
Marked.

Ray *shakes his head, then nods it.*

Ives   For life.

Pause.

Ray   See you, Ives.

Ives   Yes.

Ray *exits.* **Ives** *spits out the chewed-up piece of paper and catches it
neatly in his hand.*

Scene Two

Pete's *flat. Morning.* **Pete** *is sitting at a kitchen table.* **Ray** *enters
carrying a four-pack of beer and wearing a long old coat. He looks
dishevelled, sleepless. They look at each other.*

Ray   All right, Pete?

Pete   Yeh, I'm all right, you all right?

Ray   Yeh.

Pete   Where you been?

Ray   Oh, here and there.

Pete   Well, where? What's the matter – couldn't you sleep?

Ray   It's the room you gave me. The walls keep moving. It's
shrinking.

Pete   What d'you mean shrinking? D'you have a nightmare?

Ray   I told you. It's getting smaller. It's a nice place, Pete, but
it's definitely getting smaller.

Pete   Don't be daft. Smaller?

Ray   Where's the railway line? It was out there a minute ago.

Pete (*indicating beers*)   What's this?

Ray   D'you know I always like to know where the railway line is. Increases my sense of mobility.

Pete   Where'd you get 'em?

Ray   When does the train come?

Pete   Never mind when the train comes. Where d'you get those?

Ray   I found 'em.

Pete   Where did you find 'em?

Ray   An old man gave 'em to me.

Pete   What old man?

Ray   This old fella down by the canal. I don't know his name. I was watching the sunrise and there were lots of 'em all asleep.

Pete   What have you done?

Ray   It's all different now. Most of it's wasteland but on some they planted trees, plant boxes, little pathways.

Pete   And this fella just gave you his beers, just like that.

Ray   I was thirsty.

Pete   You didn't do anything, did you?

Ray   No. You want one?

Pete *pulls out a little phial of capsules from his pocket, shakes it.*

Pete   Just hand 'em over. Have some breakfast and take one of these.

Ray   Is it just me or are things not the same colour any more?

Pete   What d'you mean?

Ray   Green things. Green things aren't the same any more, much more faded. Yellow's not the same any more neither. And then there's the sun which is more . . . white. Silver. It's either too bright or else not even there. And the sky.

Pete   Yeh, all right, Ray . . .

Ray   Look at the sky, Pete. It's not the same. It's not even a proper blue any more. Everything is different.

Pete   Ray.

Pete *pushes the phial towards* **Ray**.

Ray   No thanks.

Pete   You have to, Ray, you know you do.

Ray   I'm not taking any more of that stuff. It addles my brain. Affects my judgment.

Ray *swigs on a beer and grins at* **Pete** *who holds out his hand for the beer.*

Pete   Give it to me.

Ray   You know what those are, Pete?

Pete   I know what they are and I know you need 'em.

Ray   Horse tranquillisers. Major knockout drops.

Pete   Just take a couple.

Ray   Chlorpromazine. Like Lithium times ten. Or a smack on the head with a claw-hammer, if you know what that's like. Hardly the elixir of life.

Pete   Listen –

Ray   I'm not listening.

Pete   If this stuff is going to keep you out of that place and stop you doing stupid things then you have to take 'em.

Ray   I don't want to.

Pete   That's not the point.

Ray   Well, what is the point?

Pause.

Have a beer with me, Pete. Let's sit down and talk about old times together.

Pete We will, Ray, but first you have to do this. If this is going to work, you have show willing.

Ray Bollocks. Since when did willing get anyone anywhere? Eh? Eh, Pete?

Pause.

Thanks for picking me up yesterday.

Pete It was a pleasure.

Ray No, I mean it. When you came to the gate in the car and you got out and opened the boot for my bags it was . . . it was a good feeling. I mean I really had that, that leaving feeling. That feeling. That feeling of leaving . . . and arriving.

Pete Good.

Ray Remember all those times when you were either picking me up from somewhere or dropping me off? Taking me to the train. Meeting me off the coach. Remember the time I got lost in Scotland? Perth. Took myself off and got arseholed with the old men of Perth for three weeks.

Pete Yeh, it was very clever.

Ray And remember the time I got lost in Wales?

Pete It's difficult to forget, Ray.

Ray Tenby. Got myself arseholed with the young people of Tenby for three weeks. All rock shops and little pubs done up to look like barns and little barns done up to look like pubs.

Pete Give us the beers, will you.

Ray Leaving and arriving, Pete, that's what I was doing. Following a pattern established over years which –

Pete The beers, Ray.

Ray Because I'm a travelling man.

Pete Ray.

Ray Swap.

Pete (*confused*) No, no swaps. I mean yes, swap.

Pete holds out the pills, Ray holds out the beers, withdrawing them as Pete tries to grab them. Eventually Pete takes the four-pack and Ray takes the phial of pills. Pete stands, puts the beers out of reach.

Ray   Hey, Pete.

Pete   Yes, Ray.

Ray   I'm sorry I never made the wedding.

Pause.

Pete   Well, you were tied up, weren't you.

Ray   I was going to be best man, wasn't I?

Pete   That's right, yeh.

Ray   I had a special little book and everything, all about what you do when you're a best man. The 'etiquette' of being a best man.

Pete   And what do you do?

Ray   I dunno. Never read it.

Pause.

And, and I'm sorry I never made the divorce neither.

Pete   You didn't miss much.

Ray   Quick, wasn't it?

Pete   Like lightning.

Ray   I mean it, Pete. I am sorry. You been growing into an old fart without me.

Pete   Well, you disappeared. Things change when you disappear.

Ray   That's what I was saying, Pete. Everything's changed. Even the . . . even the smells have changed.

Pete   Ray, listen . . .

Ray   Except for one. One smell hasn't changed.

Pete   Ray, please . . .

Ray   Remember when we was kids and we used to play in that old stream that runs underneath the brewery?

Pete   No.

Ray   Yes you do. We'd play with sticks having races. And sometimes the horses from the brewery came down and drank there. And sometimes dad came down and drank there and all, when he was working at the brewery. You remember that smell? That *mysterious* smell which we could never figure out what it was.

Pete   Horse shit.

Ray   Nah, it was a nice smell.

Pete   Ray, I've got to go to work.

Ray   I've figured out what it was. You want to know what it was, Pete? It was hops.

Pause. They look at each other.

Pete   I'm expecting deliveries. You going to go and see that woman today?

Ray *opens the phial and tosses a capsule in the air, catches it in his mouth like a peanut.*

Ray   What woman's that then?

Pete   The one they fixed you up with to sort out the thingie for your whatsit.

Ray   What whatsit?

Pete   After-sales service.

Ray *throws another capsule in the air, catches it in his mouth.*

Ray   You want one?

Pete   No thanks.

Ray   It'll calm you down.

Pete   When are you going?

Ray   I'm not going.

Pete   You're going, Ray.

Ray *shakes his head.*

Pete   Have a bath and get ready.

Ray   I didn't ask to be fixed up with any woman.

Pete   You gotta do it, Ray. The people said you gotta do it. She'll fix you up with that fella. He's supposed to be very good.

Ray   What fella?

Pete   The fella they recommended for the whatsit.

Ray (*exasperated*)   What whatsit?!

Pete (*beat*)   Observation. He's gonna help you now you're out.

Ray   Help me?

Pete   Watch you. See you don't get in any/trouble.

Ray   He's not gonna help me.

Pete   Yes he/is, Ray.

Ray   They're not here to help, these people.

Pete   They're here to –

Ray   They're here to investigate the mind.

Pete   Yes. *Your* mind.

Ray   For fun.

Pete   No, not for fun!

Ray   Because they find it interesting. They do.

Pete   Ray!

Pause. **Pete** *pulls out a ten-pound note from his pocket and hands it to* **Ray***.*

Ray   What's this?

Pete   Money.

Ray   I thought we were going to talk.

Pete   Call me when you've finished. I'll give you directions, we'll talk.

Ray   I know where it is.

Pete   Corner of Askew and –

Ray   Yeh yeh yeh off you go.

Pete *hesitates, then puts on a jacket and exits. Pause.* **Ray** *tips his head back, spits the capsules one by one into the air and catches them in his hand. Puts them back in the bottle, stands, grabs the beers and exits.*

Scene Three

The street. **Dave** *is standing over* **Laura** *who has her back against a wall.*

Dave   I'm going to count to three, Laura.

Laura   I don't know where it is!

Dave   One.

Laura   I swear, Dave, I haven't/even seen it.

Dave   Two.

Laura   Let go of/me.

Dave   I'm warning you.

Laura   What're you going to do?

Dave   Three. I'm only going to ask you this once, Laura. Once. And then I swear I'm going to get angry.

Laura   Then you're going to *get*/angry?

Dave   Where is it?

Laura   You're going to get *more*/angry.

Dave   Now I'm losing my temper.

Laura   I told you I lost it.

Dave *shoves her into the wall.*

Dave   Don't lie to me, tell me.

Laura   I don't fuckin' know where it is.

Dave   And mind your language. You got a mouth like a fuckin' sewer so you have.

Laura   Leave me alone.

Dave   You're a dirty slut. I don't need to waste my time with dirty sluts.

Laura   Then leave me alone.

Dave   I'll leave. I'll leave all right just as soon as you tell me what you did with it.

Laura   Go on get.

Dave   I am. I will. I'm gone. Believe me, boy.

Pause.

Laura   Good. Goodbye then.

Dave   You probably sold it. Sold it to pay for a holiday with your fuckin' fancy man. Is that what you did?

Laura   What fancy man?

Dave   Your little fancy man. I know you got one. To pay for your hacienda abroad with yer man there.

Laura   What haci – I don't have a fancy man.

Dave   They know I took it, Laura. Five stone sapphire. In a cluster. Not a half hoop. A cluster!

Beat.

They know I been taking stuff to give it to you.

Laura   Who?

Dave   The boys, Laura.

Laura   What 'boys'? You live in a world of your own, so you do.

Dave   The people I work for.

Laura   But you don't work!

Dave   Every job we've done I took stuff to give to you.

Laura   I don't want it.

Dave   I am trying to make you happy.

Laura   By giving me a thick ear, I suppose.

Dave   I love you, you stupid ugly cow.

Laura   That's why you put my head through a third floor window last week.

Dave   I am under pressure.

Laura   That explains it then.

Dave   They're coming after me. I am desperate.

Laura   So next time you stick my head through a window and leave me to bleed to death I'll understand.

Dave   Laura!

Pause. He takes his hands off her, brushes her shoulder with his hand. Steps back.

Just tell me who's it is. Come on, I can take it, if you tell me who's it is I promise I won't do anything. Not to you.

Laura   It's yours, Dave.

Dave   Tell me who you been getting friendly with.

Laura   I haven't been getting friendly with anybody. I don't have any friends to be friendly with.

Dave   So what am I?

Laura   Don't be stupid.

Dave   Don't call me stupid! I hate that.

Laura   I haven't been outside that stinking flat in three months. I haven't even been out to sign on.

Dave   I don't ask you to sign on still.

Laura   I like to sign on. It makes me feel normal.

Dave   I look after you.

Laura   I don't want you looking after me.

Pause.

Dave   Give me the ring and we'll call it quits.

Laura   Are you deaf?

Dave   That's all I want. Or an arm or a leg or your guts!

He slams her against the wall.

Laura   I lost it!

Dave   Where did you lose it?

Laura   If I knew that it wouldn't be lost!

Ray *wanders on and watches, unseen.*

Laura   Down the sinkhole probably.

Dave   'Probably'?

Laura   I don't know.

Dave   Well, 'probably' I'll just smash your brains out with this brick, shall I?

He stoops and picks up a loose brick, **Laura** *screams.*

Eh? Maybe I'll finish it right here. How would you like that?

Laura   Christ, help me somebody please!

Dave   Shut up!

Laura   Please!

Dave   Oh, 'please please!' D'you think they care? D'you think anybody really cares about you, Laura? Eh?

He waves the brick about.

I'll tell you something. I care about you, you don't care about me, so you know what suddenly – I don't care about you.

Laura *weeps.*

Ray   Put the brick down.

Dave *looks around in wonder. Sees* **Ray***.*

Dave   Fuck off.

Ray   No go on. You could take somebody's eye out with that thing.

Dave   What?

Ray   It's dangerous.

Dave   Is it now? And who the fuck are you?

Ray   Nobody.

Dave   That's right, pal. Mister Fucking Nobody. You wanna have a go?

Ray   Not really.

Dave *looks at* **Ray***, then* **Laura***, then* **Ray** *again, then* **Laura***.*

Dave   Wait a minute, wait a minute. (*To* **Laura***.*) Who's this?

Laura   I don't know.

Dave *heads for* **Ray** *with the brick.*

Laura   No, Dave, don't!

Dave   I'll murder the pair of you!

He flings the brick to the ground, marches up to **Ray** *and grabs him by the shirt.*

You wanna fuck with me? Eh? You wanna rescue a poor cunt in distress? Think that'll earn you brownie points?

Laura   Please, Dave, leave him alone.

Dave   Why?

Laura   I don't know why, I just think you should.

Ray   Yeh leave me alone.

Dave   Where's the ring?

Ray   I don't know what you're talking about.

Dave   Don't play games with me, cunt.

Laura   He doesn't know for Christsake! He's just some nutter.
(*To* **Ray**.) Go away. Go on.

Dave   One word of advice, nutter.

He headbutts **Ray** *who instantly collapses.*

One little gem of wisdom.

He kicks **Ray** *in the guts.*

Don't ever, never fuck with another man's misery.

(*To* **Laura**.) And if I ever catch you with another man I will kill
you. Both of you.

Dave *exits leaving* **Laura** *frozen in shock. She snaps out of it and goes to*
Ray.

Laura   O Jesus. Oh shit. What did you think you were doing?

She helps him sit up. She touches his nose.

Hello? Can you hear me? It's just a nose bleed is all. Can you feel
your nose?

Ray   Ow!

Laura   Sorry . . .

Ray *breathes hard, his breathing gets slower and slower, he cradles his*
ribs, his head hangs down, he seems to pass out.

Laura   Jesus. I'll get you to a hospital.

Ray   No! No hospitals.

Laura   You should see a doctor.

Ray   I hate doctors.

Laura (*at a loss*)   Come on then.

She gets him to his feet and they hobble off.

Scene Four

Laura's *bedsit.* **Ray** *is sitting on the bed.* **Laura** *is attending to his face.*

Ray   It's all closed up. I can't see. I'm going blind. Was that your old man then?

Laura   No.

Ray   Who is he then?

Laura   Just a fella.

Ray   Just a dangerous bloody nutter. It's funny how you never see it coming. One minute you've got your feet on the ground and the next you're five feet away staring at the stars.

Laura   You'll live.

Ray   He's not coming back, is he?

Laura   I doubt it.

Ray   Very reassuring.

Laura   You shouldn't have got involved.

Ray   He was going to kill you.

Laura   I'll be the judge of that.

Ray   He was. He said so.

Pause. **Laura** *works.*

What was he doing that for anyway?

Laura   That's my business.

Ray   He's lucky. He caught me when I wasn't looking.

Laura   You'll know to mind your own business next time.

Ray *looks at her. Pause.*

Ray   You're a bit of a hard nut, aren't you?

Laura   What d'you mean?

Ray   You don't say much. I just saved your life, you saved mine. That's not to be sneezed at. I'm only being friendly.

She works.

Laura   That's what I'm afraid of.

Ray   Why?

She sticks a sticking plaster over the bridge of his nose and steps back.

Laura   Done.

Ray   Is that it?

Laura   It'll do.

Ray   But my nose. I'm sure it's broken. Feels like his head's still up there.

Laura   D'you want to go to the hospital or not?

Ray   All right.

Laura   Can you stand?

Ray *stands shakily, pauses, then plonks back down clutching his ribs.*

Ray   No.

Laura   Try.

Ray   I just tried.

Laura   Try harder.

Ray *tries again but can't.*

Ray   It's sitting down that's done it. I shouldn't have sat down. It's like whatchmecallit, rigor mortis. I can't move my legs. I think I'm becoming a paraplegic maybe.

He rubs his ribs. She puts her hands on her hips and weighs it up.

Laura   Lift your shirt up.

Ray   What're you gonna do?

Laura   I'm gonna check your ribs. You probably cracked one.

He lifts up his T-shirt, she probes his ribs. He laughs involuntarily.

What?

Ray Cold.

She probes again. He laughs again.

Laura D'you want me to help you or not?

Ray Yeh.

Laura What's so friggin' funny then?

Ray Nothing.

Laura Does this hurt?

Ray No.

Laura This?

Ray No.

Laura This?

Ray N . . . yeh. That does.

Laura This?

Ray Up a bit . . . up a bit more. Just there. Nice.

Laura *stops instantly.*

Laura Look, if you're going to take the piss –

Ray I'm not taking the piss.

Laura You can clear off right/now.

Ray I'm not/I'm sorry.

Laura Friggin' cheek.

She packs away the Band-aids etc. in a small cabinet next to the bed, returns to **Ray**.

Laura What's the date today?

Ray I dunno, why?

Laura When were you born?

Ray August seventy-two. (*Beat.*) I'm a Leo.

Laura   I'm seeing if you're concussed or not. How's your head feel?

Ray   Are you a nurse then?

Laura   Don't be daft. I'm on the dole.

Ray   Well, for on the dole you make a great nurse. You know exactly what they do.

Laura   I think I'd rather be on the dole. Pay's better.

Ray   No, but you're an expert. How do you know all this?

Laura   Will you leave it.

Beat.

Ray   What about this place then, is it yours?

Laura   It's council, I rent it.

Ray   Does he live here too then, whatshisname?

Laura   No, he doesn't – now do you think you can stand up?

Ray   Does he often do this sort of thing?

Laura   Would you stop asking awkward questions.

Ray   Scrape you up against walls, fling bricks at people it's not/nice.

Laura   If you don't mind –

Ray   It's rude.

Laura   I think it's time you were on your/way.

Ray   I've met his sort before. Got nothing better to do than go round whacking people and scaring the shit out of them. You see them walking around wired, angry, wound up ready to ping. He probably practises. It's not the first time this has happened to me, you know. It's not the first time I've completely unwittingly provoked somebody. I just –

Laura   If it's all the same to you –

Ray   Say the wrong thing or look at them the wrong way. People like this do not like to be looked at. It's instinctive. And it's like –

Laura   If I could just get a word in/edgeways.

Ray   Pardon me for being so bold as to exchange a look in the street while I'm going about my business, pardon me for daring to speak to you because we do not speak to each other.

Laura   I'm trying.

Ray   We just don't, not if we are complete strangers.

Laura   Are you listening?

Ray   And it's like/what –

Laura   Jesus Mary and Joseph!

Ray   Is your problem, pal? That's what I say.

Pause.

Laura   I have to go out. I don't want to be rude but I have an important appointment and so I have to go out.

Ray   Will I see you again?

Laura   What kind of question's that?

Pause. **Ray** *gets up.*

Ray   Makes sense to me.

Laura   It would do, wouldn't it.

Ray   I'm sorry.

Laura   So am I.

Ray   I'm going.

Laura   Thank you.

Ray   Out the door.

Laura   Thank you.

Ray *goes to the door.*

Ray   I'm going out the door now.

Laura   Thank you very much.

Ray   You're welcome. Are you going to be/all right?

Laura   What? Yeh fine.

Ray   Fine then.

Ray *nods and exits.*

Scene Five

The restaurant kitchen. Spanish guitar music plays. **Pete** *is preparing two plates of food on a prep table.* **Ray** *watches, his face bandaged and eye black.*

Pete   What the fuck happened?

Ray   Nothing happened.

Pete   What happened to your face?

Ray   Nothing happened to my face.

Pete   You shot your mouth off again, didn't you?

Ray   No.

Pete   Look at yourself, Ray. Christ.

He examines **Ray***'s face.*

This is a serious fuck up. A serious one. I leave you alone five minutes and you're in trouble.

Ray   I'm not, Pete.

Pete   Yes, Ray, this is what I call trouble. What would you call it?

Ray   An accident.

Pete   You cannot afford to get into trouble. How can I impress this upon you? Because if you get into trouble I get into trouble. They'll come to me and they'll see this and they'll think what?

Ray   I dunno, what?

Pete What do you think they'll think? They'll think you're in trouble that's what they'll think.

Ray Maybe they'll think it was an/accident too.

Pete Because the patient's brother, this person to whom we've entrusted him to, cannot be trusted. And nor can the patient. And so they put you away again.

Ray (*beat*) It's quite a long/story.

Pete I signed a form. I signed a bit of paper to get you out of that place. They said 'Let's let him out, let's send him back to his family – even though he doesn't have a family any more we'll find somebody' and they found me. I haven't seen you in years, I don't even know who you are any more but, fuck, yes I'm here for you, Ray, and I put that in writing we go through a whole procedure and you don't . . . appear to give a shit.

Ray I do give a/shit, Pete.

Pete Don't tell me you walked into a door. Always walking into doors, weren't you? You'd vanish off the face of the earth and walk into a door somewhere.

He speaks into an intercom on the wall.

Two curly sausages for table five.

He takes two plates to a serving hatch and puts them down.

Got yourself arrested. Did you get arrested again?

Ray I didn't get arrested, honestly.

Pete You been beaten up – how else do you explain it? Why don't you just move into Hammersmith nick? You used to practically live there. Either that or me or mum God rest her soul would be knocked up at all hours by the police cos they found you in some heap somewhere. You could be dead for all I know but all you think about is me me me . . . (*Into intercom.*) Two curly sausages for table five what the hell's going on?

Intercom Sorry, guv.

Pete (*to* **Ray**) Oh no, Pete, I'm all right, Jack-the-Lad I am. The wind changed and my face turned to pulp by itself.

Ray   Are you listening to me?

Pete   You can't live like that again, Ray, you're not up to it. You understand? (*Beat.*) It's what sent you screwy in the first place.

Ray   Nothing 'sent me screwy'.

Pete   Well, it hardly helped, did it?

Ray   Nothing 'sent' me screwy, Pete. Nothing sent me.

Pete   I just don't understand it that's all I just . . . don't understand.

Ray   Nobody understands it.

Pete   Why can't you just . . . pull yourself together?

Ray   Pull myself together.

Pete   Something like that, yeh. (*Into intercom.*) Two curly sausages for –

Intercom   Curly sausage.

Pete   What?

Intercom   Curly sausage, yeh?

Pete   Yes curly –

Intercom   Not Polish?

Pete   No, not Polish Spiced –

Intercom   They want pizza –

Pete   Well, they can't have pizza –

Intercom   They changed their minds –

Pete   Tell 'em to make up their bloody minds.

Ray   How do I pull myself together, Pete? Is there a string or something that people just pull on every time they're in the shit?

Pete   You know what I mean.

Ray   Yes I do and I don't fucking like it.

Pete (*into intercom*)   The curly fucking sausages are getting curly fucking cold all right? (*To* **Ray**.) I employ imbeciles. It's cheaper but it has its drawbacks.

He starts preparing another two plates.

My kitchen hand is unwell, probably hung over. I'll sack him tomorrow.

Ray   Are you listening, Pete?

They look at each other.

Pete   I'm sorry. You'll have to be patient with me, OK? You have to be patient with me I have to be patient with you.

Long pause as **Pete** *works.*

Ray   You want a hand?

Pete   I'll be all right.

Ray   I could wash up the plates.

Pete   I've got an imbecile to do that.

Ray   Remember when dad was here and I used to wash up? Chief dishwasher. It was his dream to have a place like this, wasn't it?

Pete   I dunno, was it?

Ray   It was. All that simple stuff he was doing, bacon, beans, omelette, he couldn't give it away, could he?

Pete   I still do that during the day.

Ray   And at night you do this. What is it? Italian? He liked Italian.

Pete   Mediterranean. Pizzas and curly sausage. Gourmet pizzas like with smoked salmon and artichoke hearts. Sour cream. The yuppies love it. (*Into intercom*.) Ask table seven if they're ready to order and interest them in the fish soup.

Silence.

Intercom   Why?

Pete   Because I made fish soup today and if I don't get rid of it those fish'll start swimming again. (*To* **Ray**.) Sorry, where were we?

Ray   I could persuade 'em to have the soup.

Pete   Did you go and see that woman today?

Ray   Which woman?

Pete   Did you?

Ray   Yeh.

Pete   Because it's important, you know that.

Ray   I know that.

Pete   What did she say?

Ray   Said keep up the good work and come back in two weeks.

Pete   Two weeks, why two weeks?

Ray   Why not two weeks?

Pete   Was your face like that when you went to see her?

Ray   No, why?

Pete   Because if it was then she wouldn't have said that, would she? It'd be a different kettle of fish altogether. (*Into intercom.*) Pesto pizza pie for table four.

Ray *takes a plate to the hatch, puts it down.*

Pete   What did happen to your face, Ray?

Ray   What's pesto pizza pie?

Pete   It's pesto and pizza . . . in a pie. Now just tell me/what –

Ray   In a pie?

Pete   Folded over like a pie, yeh, not many people do it . . .

Ray   I'm not surprised.

Pete   Ray, I haven't got all night.

Ray (*beat*)   I met this girl. Her old man was giving her a hard time – I mean a really hard time, Pete.

Pete   Oh, Ray, you didn't –

Ray   So I –

Pete   You stuck your nose in.

Ray   He was gonna brick her face. I told him to stop.

Pete   Oh, good plan, Ray, I'm sure that worked/a treat.

Ray   Quite freaked me at the/time.

Pete   Never get involved.

Ray   He was murdering her!

Pete   That's not your problem.

Ray   I didn't know what to do.

Pete   It's her problem. Every person has their own set of problems. Every person has a hand of cards they are dealt in this life. If somebody has a bad card you don't pick up their bad card.

Ray   Yeh, but murder, Pete –

Pete   You have your own bad cards.

Ray   Puts a different slant on things.

Pete   What are you doing tomorrow?

Ray   I dunno.

Pete   Yes you do know, Ray, because I just told you. Didn't I just tell you? You go and see the woman and you do what she tells you to do.

Ray   Yes, Pete.

Pete   And you do what I tell you to do.

Ray   Yes, Pete.

Pete   And you do what they told me to tell you to do. All right?

Ray   All right, Pete. But, Pete, I mean I just feel, Pete –

Pete   Ray Ray Ray – everybody feels. We all have feelings but we don't let them rule our lives. (*Beat.*) Are you hungry?

Ray   Starved.

Pete   Clear a space.

Ray *clears a space on the prep table.* **Pete** *goes to the service hatch.*

Ray   But what am I gonna do with my time besides all that?

Pete   We'll cross that bridge when we come to it.

Ray   We have come to it.

Pete   Give it one more try. Eh? (*Beat.*) Have you ever had curly sausage before?

Ray   No.

Pete   Well, today is your lucky day.

He plonks the plate down in front of **Ray**. **Ray** *looks at it.*

And tomorrow will be my lucky day if you do what you're supposed to. Is that a deal?

Ray   It's a deal.

Pete   Eat your grub.

Pete *gets back to work.* **Ray** *stares at his plate.*

Ray   Pete?

Pete   Yes?

Ray   What's curly sausage?

Pete   It's just sausage, Ray. It's just like straight sausage only it's curly.

Ray (*eating*)   Nice.

Pete   It's got spices in it, I dunno, herbs or something.

Ray   Tastes good.

Pete   Yeh?

Ray   Yeh.

Pete   Good.

Scene Six

The pub. A few days later. **Laura** *is sitting at a table drinking and smoking a cigarette. Music blasts out.* **Ray** *wanders over with drink in hand.*

Ray   Is . . . is anybody sitting there?

Laura   Only if they're very small.

Ray   Can I sit there?

Laura *shrugs.* **Ray** *sits.*

Ray   All right?

Pause.

It's nice here. (*Beat.*) All my friends come here. (*Beat.*) They're not here at the moment.

Laura   I like it.

Ray   It's a friendly place. I like the music they play. It's not old and it's not new. Very few pubs play this type of music nowadays. Are you Irish?

Laura   What?

Ray   This is an Irish pub.

Laura   I'm from Limerick.

Ray   Did you know that there is more drunkenness, suicide and madness amongst the Irish in London than any other race on earth?

Laura   Is that so?

Ray   Yes, well, that's what they say because mostly you see they're away from their family and they're lonely probably and sometimes there's prejudice against 'em because of who they are and they can't get jobs and things but also mainly it's just loneliness. Have you got any family here or are you just on your own?

Laura   I'm on my own.

Ray   Me too. I just got my brother. Me dad vanished some years ago but there's still my brother. My mother's dead. Cancer I believe.

Pause.

No cats, no dogs, no — what are they — little hairy things, in a cage . . . I don't have any sisters. Do you have any sisters?

Laura   Yeh, I've got a couple of sisters.

Ray   And do you like them?

Laura   They're all right.

Ray   That's good because you have to be able to like your family. You have to be able to trust them but mainly you have to like them. And sometimes you just don't. Sometimes you don't trust anybody. Then again sometimes you form a vague attachment/to —

Laura   I have no idea, no idea at all, what you are talking about. Can you see that?

Pause.

Ray   Would you like a drink?

Laura   Look, I'm sorry if it looked like I wanted you to sit down but in fact I really didn't. What I wanted was to be left alone. And I'm not just saying that, I mean it. I don't want to talk to anybody I don't want to see anybody I don't want to fight with anybody I don't want to drink with anybody smile at anybody play Let's Get To Know Each Other I just don't want to know. I'm in a bad mood.

Ray   Well, why'd you come here?

Laura   Because . . . I'm in a bad mood. Why did you come here?

Ray (*beat*)   I was bored.

Laura   You were bored so you thought you'd come and talk to me.

Ray *shrugs. Pause.*

Ray It's nice here. I live round here. My brother he runs a restaurant it's very busy, sometimes I help out.

Laura Really.

Ray Yes, all the time. (*Beat.*) No, never. What happened to your face?

Laura What?

Ray You/all right?

Laura Nothing happened.

Ray That doesn't look like nothing to me. You got quite a shiner. And your lip's all cut. And your arm, look at your arm.

Laura I fell out of bed.

Ray Ah, I'm always falling out of bed. Falling out of bed and walking into doors. You want to get some carpet in that place that way you won't bruise so easy. So so so did you get to your appointment?

Laura *looks at him then glances around the pub uneasily.*

Laura Yes, thank you.

Ray You must be up the spout then. Am I right?

Laura I beg your pardon?

Ray Is it his then? That fella of yours?

Laura Yes it's his all his handiwork just like your nose. Any other/questions?

Ray I'm surprised people still want to have babies. I find it fascinating. I mean they say you get a special glow and everything when you have a baby. Like a special . . .

She gets up.

Laura I have to go.

Ray Please stay, sit down don't get all –

Ray *gets up and puts a hand on her arm, she bats it away.*

Laura Don't touch me!

Ray Sorry!

Laura What is wrong with you?

Ray I just want to get to know you a bit, what's wrong with that?

Laura You don't get to know somebody by just walking up to them in a pub and talking absolute friggin' rubbish to them for half an hour.

Ray What d'you want me to do?

Laura Are you simple or wha'?

Ray I offered you a drink.

Laura That is not how it happens.

Ray Well, how does it happen?

Laura I don't know!

Ray You don't believe me, do you? I like you. I'm not being funny. I thought you liked me seeing as I saved your life and all. I can't do that every day you know, my brother ain't half got the hump. He don't believe me neither.

Pause. **Laura** *sighs and sits.*

Ray You got nice eyes.

Laura I don't believe this.

Ray Incredible blue like two swimming pools.

Laura You don't give up, do you?

Ray Not really/no.

Laura I'm not going to sleep with you, you know.

Ray What?

Laura I said . . . (*Lowers her voice.*) I'm not going to sleep with you. If that's what you're getting at.

Ray I don't want you to sleep with me.

Laura It's out of the question.

Ray   I didn't ask you to sleep/with me.

Laura   Because, because –

Ray   I don't want you to sleep/with me.

Laura   I'm not sleeping with/anybody.

Ray   I don't want you/to.

Laura   Just at the moment. Sleeping with people is not the answer to/anything.

Ray   I don't want you to sleep with me.

Pause.

Laura   And I'm not doing anything else either.

Ray   I don't want you to.

Laura   Nothing, you understand? Nothing.

Ray   I don't want to.

Pause. They look around sheepishly.

Laura   Well, good. I'm glad we got that sorted/out.

Ray   Who said anything about sleeping with you?

Laura   I just thought that might have been where things were heading.

Ray   Course not. (*Beat.*) I don't like sleeping anyway, it's boring. I've been asleep for too long.

Laura   You know that's not what/I meant.

Ray   I can't sleep, at night my brother says, 'Go to sleep,' and I can't. I don't want to. I have nightmares.

Pause.

Laura   What d'you have nightmares about?

Ray   Strange things. Things are always the wrong colour or the wrong size. Things speaking to me. Like birds. I mean real birds that fly.

Laura   What's so scary about that? I'd love to have nightmares about birds.

Ray   I scare easily. Well, I can't speak to them, can I? I'm not Doctor fuckin' Doolittle. (*Beat. She laughs a little.*) What about yours?

Laura   Who said I get 'em?

Ray   You must do.

Laura   Yeh, well . . . I wake up before anything really bad happens.

Ray   I know that sort and all. Awful.

Laura   Yeh . . . awful.

Pause.

I'm/sorry I –

Ray   No, I'm/sorry.

Laura   I didn't/mean to –

Ray   I just barged/in –

Laura   No you –

Ray   I –

Laura   I –

Ray   I'll get the drinks in.

Laura   Get the drinks in good idea.

Ray   A pint is it?

Laura   Vodka. Double.

Ray *gets up hurriedly and goes to the bar.* **Laura** *smokes her cigarette. Pause. She fidgets.* **Ray** *returns and plonks a vodka orange and a beer down.*

Ray   You shouldn't smoke and drink you know.

Laura   There's a lot of things I shouldn't do.

Ray   But you still do 'em. Me too. I personally like to live as if I'm gonna die tomorrow.

Laura   You might do.

Ray   Yeh, yes that's exactly it. That's exactly it.

Pause.

I'm Ray, by the way.

Laura   Laura.

He puts his hand out, they shake. Beat.

Ray   Can I have a feel?

Laura   What?

Ray   Of your . . . of the . . .

He indicates her belly.

Laura   Of this?

Ray *nods.* **Ray** *puts his hand on her belly.* **Laura** *looks straight ahead.* **Ray** *puts his ear to her belly and listens.* **Laura** *looks around awkwardly.*

Scene Seven

Split scene. **Ray** *is in a telephone box at the seaside, the sound of gulls overhead and waves.* **Laura** *strolls about outside throwing chips from a bag at the gulls.* **Pete** *is in his kitchen talking on the wall phone.*

Ray   Pete.

Pete   Ray, is that you?

Ray   Pete, it's me.

Pete   Where are you?

Ray   Can you hear me?

Pete   I can hear you, Ray, where are you calling from?

Ray *turns to* **Laura**, *opens the door a crack.*

Ray   Where are we?

Laura   Southend.

Ray   Southend.

Pete   Southend? What are you doing in Southend?

Ray   I came to see the sea. Get away from it all.

Pete   Who are you with?

Ray   I met a girl.

Pete   What?

Ray   You know. A woman.

Pete   Don't fuck me about, Ray. I'm not kidding.

Ray   Nor am I. I met someone, a bird, a chick, a little tweetie-pie –

Pete   All right I get the message – who?

Ray   Her name's Laura.

Pete   Yeh and?

Ray   Lives up near the canal. Up Harlesden way. She's got her own place. It's a nice place, Pete.

Pete   How did you meet her?

Ray   You'd like her.

Pete   How did you meet this person, Ray?

Ray   Does it matter?

Pete   Yes it does matter.

Ray   I was just hanging around and she was hanging around and our paths just crossed.

Pete   You met her in the pub.

Ray   No/I swear.

Pete   You bloody fool, what on earth do you think you're doing?

Ray   Remember how I told you about the –

Pete   No more stories, Ray, I'm not/listening.

Ray   This bloke right –

Pete   Just come home.

Ray   And now he's –

Pete   Now.

Pause.

Ray   You don't believe me, do you?

Pete   Oh, I believe you all right.

Ray   Do you want to speak to her?

He leans out of the phone box.

He wants to speak to you.

Pete   Ray, it's just fast work that's all.

Ray   It's a fast world, Pete. Sometimes things happen even too fast for even you to understand.

Pete   Oh, is that so? (*Beat.*) Listen, Ray, are you sure you didn't . . . blackout or something?

Ray   Positive, Pete.

Pete   Because it wouldn't be the first time, would it?

Ray   No it wouldn't but I'm fine. I'm dandy in fact you could say I'm well chuffed. I like it here. It's like I'm in a movie, you know? All the people on the beach drink beers out of plastic cups and they play nineteen-fifties music.

Pete   You haven't been taking your medication, have you?

Ray   What's that?

Pete   Your pills. You left 'em here, you hardly touched 'em.

Ray   I forgot.

Pete   Jesus!

Pause.

Ray   You still there, Pete?

Pete When are you coming home?

Ray I dunno. I might stay a while, we been having a wicked/ time.

Pete Get on a train and come home. I got enough to deal with without you wandering off again. D'you want me to come and get you?

Ray We'll be all right.

Pete No, I'm coming to get you. Where are you?

Ray What's that?

Pete What's the name of the street.

Ray *makes static noises with his mouth, pulls a crisp wrapper from his pocket and ruffles it against the phone.*

Ray I can't hear you, Pete . . . it's breaking up . . . bad line . . . I . . . oh no.

Pete Ray? Ray! Hello?

Ray *hangs up the phone.* **Pete** *listens for a moment then slams the phone down.* **Ray** *gets out of the phone box, lights a fag and looks around happily.* **Laura** *comes over, he gives her a fag and lights it up. Lights down slowly on* **Pete** *as he paces.*

Laura What did he say?

Ray Said stay as long as we like.

Laura Do you always have to ring him when you go somewhere?

Ray He gets bored. I just ring to cheer him up.

Laura Are you sure he's OK about it? Sounds like you might have some explaining to do.

Ray Nah, he just worries too much. Worries I might accidently enjoy myself. He's like an old woman sometimes.

Laura Well, I think it must be nice to have somebody to worry about you like that.

Ray It's a drag. Let's go on the pier.

Laura We been on the pier all day for goodness sake!

Ray We'll go again. I like the pier.

He grabs her hand and tows her away.

Scene Eight

Tube station. **Ives** *stands with shopping bags of belongings, drinking from a beer can and examining the note* **Ray** *gave him.* **Dave** *walks towards the tube dressed in a black suit and white shirt, top button done up, clean-shaven. He stops, turns and stares in the direction he's just come from, puffing on a cigarette.*

Ives Psst.

Dave *ignores him.*

Ives Psst.

Dave Get lost.

Dave *continues searching.*

Ives The corner of Uxbridge and Askew.

Dave What about it?

Ives Where is it?

Dave Have you seen a girl come out of that pub there?

Ives Are you local?

Dave Have you? Red hair. Skinny.

Ives It's important.

Dave Have you?

Ives No.

Dave *checks his cuffs and collar and goes on staring.*

Ives I'm lost.

Dave Everybody's lost. Now leave me alone before I break your fuckin' legs off.

Beat.

Ives   That's a nice suit.

Beat.

Bespoke.

Dave   Yeh yeh.

Ives   Nice.

Dave   Yeh.

Ives   I had a suit once.

Dave *ignores him.*

Ives   Tailored. Five inch vents. Three buttons. All the rage.
You can respect a man in a suit and the ladies like it too.
Wear A Suit Today And Keep Heartache At Bay.
Once I Had A Secret Love and all because I wore a suit.

Dave   You're a bit old for that kind of talk, aren't you?

Ives   My old man swore by them.

Dave   I look all right then?

Ives   Beautiful, man, beautiful.

Dave   Yeh?

Ives   I had a friend and then he scarpered.

Dave *snatches the note off* **Ives**, *reads it and points.*

Dave   Straight ahead. Through the market.

Ives   Thank you.

Ives *moves to go,* **Dave** *stops him with a restraining arm.*

Dave   Then left.

Ives   Right.

Dave   Then straight on. Then left.

Ives *moves again.* **Dave** *stops him.*

Dave   There's a kind of a . . . kink in the road. Watch for the
kink. It'll be there for you somewhere.

Ives Thank you.

Dave Any time.

Ives Have a Guinness.

Dave G'way with yer.

Ives You need it.

Dave I said no, OK?

Pause.

I'll go stark staring if I don't find her, you know that, don't you?

Beat.

D'you believe me?

Beat. **Ives** *drinks.*

I'll wind up like you. Fuck me.

He digs into his pocket, pulls out a fiver, hands it to **Ives**.

Go on get out of my sight. Get lost.

Scene Nine

A field, **Ray** *and* **Laura** *are on a blanket holding each other, not speaking. There is food and a bottle of wine and a four-pack beside them.* **Ray** *strokes* **Laura**'s *cheek.*

Laura You know we shouldn't be doing this. (*Beat.*) You could be some type of maniac. (*Beat.*) I could be some type of maniac. (*Beat.*) So why are we doing it?

Ray We're just stupid I guess.

They kiss.

Wow.

Laura Yes, wow.

Ray You're a good kisser.

Laura Yeh, well . . .

Ray Has anybody ever told you that?

Laura No. I mean yeh, so are you.

Ray You got nice big lips.

He puckers his mouth experimentally.

Nice and firm. What shall we do now?

She breaks away, folds her knees under her chin. **Ray** *chews on a piece of straw.*

Laura I didn't want this to happen, you know that, don't you?

Ray Yeh.

Laura I've only just escaped from the last man I was with.

Ray You can't keep escaping forever otherwise you'll run out of places to escape to.

Laura Depends on what you're escaping from. When I say escape I mean really escape. Like jump out of windows and dig tunnels type of escape that's what I'm talking about.

Ray Mm.

Laura I mean, I thought I had escaped. This is me escaping. I escape all right but he just keeps coming back.

Ray Persistent.

Laura Yes.

Ray Why?

Laura He has to be with me the whole time or something. He goes mad if he's not with me. I go mad if he is.

Ray Is that why he hit you?

Laura I don't know why he hit me.

Ray Maybe he couldn't . . . couldn't express himself or something.

Laura Maybe he just likes hitting people.

Ray Maybe he was confused.

Laura I was confused but it's no excuse to –

Ray Maybe he loved you so much . . . that he just hit you.

Laura   What on *earth* are you talking about?

Pause.

Ray   No, maybe not. (*Beat.*) You must've liked him once.

Laura (*sighs*)   He could be quite charming when he wanted to be so. Well . . . not so much charming. Persuasive, I suppose.

Ray   What about when he hit you?

Laura   Oh, he could be very persuasive then.

Ray   But you stayed with him.

Laura   You get used to it after a while.

Ray   How can you get used to it?

Laura   You don't expect it to . . . keep happening, I suppose. (*Beat.*) He was always after calling me a slut or a whore and then the next minute I was frigid. He'd accuse me of going with other men, then he'd say I'd never find another man who'd have me. (*Beat.*) If someone says something like that often enough, you find yourself believing it. It's a miracle the things you find yourself believing.

Ray   I know what you mean.

Laura   I used to worry that I was going a bit mad because I still liked him. I'd get lonely without him and miss him because sometimes at night he could be something warm to get up against or something. When we'd been together his skin and his hands would always be warm . . . but when he came in after a night out he was cold, I mean his hands were cold his . . . knuckles. At first he could make things feel different. But then he couldn't.

Pause.

Ray   Couldn't you go somewhere? Go home?

Laura   They say I cause trouble.

Ray   I've heard that before and all.

Laura   I don't need anyone telling me how to redeem my mistakes.

Pause.

Ray   What d'you think would happen if we stayed here and didn't go back?

Laura   Stayed here in this field?

Ray   Yeh.

Laura   (*shrugs*)   We'd die of starvation probably.

Pause.

Ray   Kiss me.

They kiss chastely. Beat. They kiss passionately and fall back on the rug. He kisses her neck and chest wildly, peppering her with kisses. She giggles.

Laura   Euch, stop! (*He does.*) No keep going. Here . . . on my mouth.

He kisses her on the mouth.

Now squash me. On top. I want to feel your weight.

He climbs on top.

Ray   Like this?

Laura   Harder. Squeeze the breath out of me.

He does so.

Harder!

He wriggles and laughs.

Ray   Why?

Laura   Makes me feel safe.

They lie like that for a moment. **Ray** *kisses her neck, starts unbuttoning her dress.*

Ray   You've got beautiful breasts, Laura. I want to suck them.

They kiss, he puts his hand between her legs.

Laura   Bit higher . . . down . . . just there.

Blackout.

Act Two

Scene One

Pete's *flat.* **Ray, Ives** *and* **Pete** *sit around the kitchen table.* **Ives** *and* **Ray** *drink beers.*

Ives (*singing loudly*)   'I wish I was in London or some other seaport town I'll set myself on a steam boat and I'll sail the ocean round,'

Ray (*simultaneously*)   De da de da de da . . .

Ives   'While sailing round the ocean while sailing round the sea I'd dream of handsome Molly wherever she might be,'

Ray   Join in Pete – 'Wherever she might be,'

Ives   'Her hair's as black as raven her eyes as black as coal her teeth are like the lilies,'

Ray (*simultaneously*)   Da da de da . . .

Ives   'That in the morning glow!'

Pete   I don't think I can take much more of this.

Ives   'And now you've gone and left me go on with who you please,'

Pete   Enough!

Ives   'My poor heart is aching . . .'

Ray   Ives, schtum.

Pause.

Pete   So . . . Ives, you were at Epsom with Ray?

Ives   Ah, yes, he's a good boy, lovely fella.

Pete   And . . . how long have you been back in London?

Ray   He got out just after me.

Ives   Escaped.

Ray   Escaped just after me.

Pete   And you're living round here?

Ives   That's right. Underneath the arches. (*Singing loudly.*) 'Underneath the arches . . .'

Ray   Under the bridge. The flyover, isn't that right, Ives?

Ives   I, I, I, I, I, I'm not from round here no. I come from far away. A distant and very beautiful planet, the Planet Vega as a matter of fact.

Pete   I see.

Pause.

So . . . where is this Planet Vega, then?

Ives   Don't patronise me. Do you think it's funny?

Pete   No.

Ives (*to* **Ray**)   Does he?

Ray   I don't think so.

Ives   Do you?

Ray   Of course not.

Ives   It's not my fault. They came and got me, I didn't go to them. They took me away, took me to their leader. He told me all about you. Described you perfectly. (*To* **Pete**.) Especially you.

Pete   Really?

Ives   I was in the gasworks before that. Sixteen years in the gasworks and the whole fucking lot goes sky high. Explosion. I was there, I saw the missiles go up. High into the sky they went and on the ground a great flaming fireball. No safety precautions on account of the fact they wanted it to happen, you understand? They sent the missiles up as a signal. Why? To let them know I was ready. Why? Because they wanted to get rid of me.

Pause.

Pete   Why would they want to get rid of you?

Ives   To save on early retirement. One month off early retirement I was. One month. Now look at me. There's not enough room any more. They want us all to go away!

Pete   I'm sure they don't.

Ives   What would you know about it? Look at you with your little baby-arsed face scrubbed clean and beautiful.

Pete   Ray –

Ives   I shall tell you what I think about the monied classes. They are the progenitors of beauty. The rich copulate with the beautiful and they breed. They breed more rich and beautiful. I do not like to be told that beauty is within because beauty is a commodity. I do not like to hear people say money is no obstacle because money is the obstacle. I don't need to be told as long as you have your health because you buy your health and so it is a question of as long as you can afford it. I'm not stupid. I can think. I can see the people that pass me by.

Pause.

Pete   Can I have a quiet word, Ray?

Ives   Hey you yes you! I'm talking to you.

Pete *and* **Ray** *get up and move a short distance away.* **Ives** *stands on his chair.*

Ives   THERE IS NO REVOLUTION! THERE NEVER WILL BE BECAUSE YOU ARE NOT THE REVOLUTIONARY TYPE!

Pete   Get him out of here.

Ives   NEVER IN THIS COUNTRY WILL THERE BE ANYTHING THAT SMACKS OF JUSTICE!

Pete   Enough is enough. This is my home.

Ray   Where's he gonna go?

Pete   Take him to a hostel or something. The Novotel – anywhere.

Pete *pulls out a wad of notes from his pocket and hands* **Ray** *a couple.*

Ives   You can't buy me.

Ray   It's not that easy, Pete.

Ives   You could make me an offer but I wouldn't think about it.

Pete   It is that easy. I want him out and I want you to deal with it. It's not too complicated even for you.

Ray   I said he could stay over. Stop here/for a while.

Pete   What?!

Beat. They look at each other. **Ives** *climbs down.*

Ives (*to* **Pete**)   I remember you.

Pete   Oh, Jesus . . .

Ives   You and this area and everybody here from when I was small . . .

Pete (*simultaneously, ignoring* **Ives**)   Are you insane? What are you trying to do to me?

Ives   My old mum she used to take us to the Bishop's Park as it was known then/when it was sunny . . .

Pete   I can't do it! I can't help! OK? Don't you understand?

Ives   The golden mile we trekked to the Bishop's Park where they had a lagoon with a little fake island/in the middle like a pot plant . . .

Ray   You'll get used to it, Pete.

Pete   It's blowing my circuits! He stinks, Ray. He won't shut up. It's like being in a . . . fuckin' lunatic asylum!

Silence. **Ives** *stands, drains his beer, pats his pockets, gathers up two more empty cans, shakes them and moves to the door.*

Ives   . . . I'm sorry.

Ray   Wait, Ives . . .

Ives *exits.* **Pete** *sighs and sits at the table. Pause.*

Pete You know, Ray . . . if you wanna piss your life away then fine but don't piss mine away too. You . . . see what I'm saying?

Pause. **Ray** *sits at the table.* **Pete** *picks up a can from the table, crushes it and throws it back.*

Pete This is just what dad used to do.

Ray Is it now.

Pete That's how he pissed his caff away, pissed it all away drinking.

Ray He was a drunk. That's what drunks do.

Pete You never went through with him what I went through. Is that how you wanna end up? Is it?

Pause. **Pete** *pulls out the phial of pills from his pocket and plonks them on the table.* **Ray** *grabs them.*

Ray I been looking for those everywhere.

Pete Do I have to stand over you morning and night every night for the rest of your life? (*Beat.*) For the rest of your life, Ray.

Ray *shrugs.*

Pete And . . . for the rest of my life. I mean how weird are things gonna get? You been out two weeks and you haven't done any of the things you're supposed to do. I'm keeping my end of the deal what about yours?

Ray Don't talk to me about deals – I'm not doing any more deals.

Pete You want me to force you, is that it?

Ray How you gonna force me?

Pete I don't know, Ray. I'm sure I'll think of something.

Ray Drugs are bad for you, Pete. Everybody knows that.

Pete Not these ones! Jesus.

Ray They lead to worser things.

Pete   Oh, like what? Like . . . him? Do you wanna end up under a bridge as well?

Ray   I'm weaning myself off 'em.

Pete   What?

Ray   Going for a more natural approach. I need a whatisit . . . stable environment. Need to be around people I know and can trust and all that.

Pete   But you never are around, Ray, I never know where you are! Where do you go? Where have you . . . Where have you been?

Ray   With Laura. I told you.

Pete   Oh, don't start that again.

Ray   'Don't start'? Don't start what again?

Beat.

You still don't believe me, do you?

Beat.

I'm tired of living here.

Pete   Why?

Ray   You got noisy neighbours. Every damn night I hear them revving up their fancy cars and popping champagne corks. What's the matter, Pete, you grown out of the Bush? You in a different bracket now so you don't notice things any more?

Pete   What am I supposed to notice?

Ray   These . . . *arseholes.* I've seen them trotting about in their tennis outfits with their dolly birds with the sunbed tans. I've seen them go where the sunbeds are and come back orange. They're probably all your customers. It's disgusting. What I need is a gun, a Sten gun, that'd put a few holes in their party frocks.

Pause.

Pete   Jesus, Ray, they're only –

Ray   Fuckers.

Pete   They're my neighbours.

Ray   It's doing my head in.

Pete   They're just people.

Pete   People do my head in.

Pause.

Pete   You mean . . . 'doing your head in' or actually doing your head in?

Ray   I mean it gets on my tits.

Pete   Well, Ray, you don't have to live here. You don't have to do any of this. Nor do I. I mean . . . (*Beat.*) Maybe you could get your own place. Bedsit or something. That's the idea, isn't it? Get you on your own two feet. (*Beat.*) I mean they can't expect you to stay here forever. Can they?

Ray   I'm going to Laura's.

Pete   Are you now.

Ray   Yeh.

Pete   Oh well, Jesus, why the hell not – you been going out with her for a whole two weeks. Good idea.

Beat.

You're serious, aren't you? There really is a Laura?

Ray   Yeh.

Pete   And that's where you been staying?

Ray   What's wrong with that?

Pete (*beat*)   OK, well then, maybe we should do something. (*Beat.*) Talk to them about it. (*Beat.*) We'll go in there and tell 'em there's a change in plan. Fuck their plan, it isn't working, there's a new one. Why not?

Ray   I already have.

Pete   What?

Ray   She said it's a good idea too.

Pete (*laughs*)   Just like that. Just like that she said, 'Go ahead, shack up with this bird enjoy yourself.'

Ray   That's right, more or less exactly what she said.

Pete   You actually went to see her?

Ray   Yeh, she had a . . . mole on her lip.

Pete (*sotto voce*)   I don't believe it . . .

Pause.

Ray   It's going to be all right, Pete.

Pete   Come on, Ray, this is stupid. It's stupid!

Ray   Don't worry about it.

Pete   I can't help worrying about it.

Ray   You have a business to run.

Pete   I know, yes I know that –

Ray   And there's nothing you can do anyway.

They look at each other.

Scene Two

Laura's *flat. Morning. The telephone is ringing.* **Ray** *and* **Laura** *are sitting up in bed.* **Ray** *is smoking a cigarette. After a while he leans over, picks up the receiver and hangs it up. Pause.* **Laura** *takes* **Ray**'s *hand and places it on her belly.*

Laura   Feel.

She plonks **Ray**'s *hand on her belly.*

He'll be wanting to come out soon enough. He'll be walking about and talking and expecting to learn things. What am I going to teach him?

Pause.

Ray   I never thought of it like that.

Laura   I dreamt that I'd already had it. It was tiny. About the size of my thumb and it was blue. Blue and white and red and made of plastic. With . . . some kind of light on it and the light said whether it was still alive. I carried it round on the bus with me waiting to tell somebody but I was too afraid. I worked out that the light meant how warm it was and I was afraid I didn't have enough warmth. I went into a pub and had a drink and when I came out . . . the light had gone out. And it was dead. I felt so ashamed.

Pause.

Ray   Which pub?

Laura   Ray!

Ray   What?

She hits him with a pillow.

Laura   You're supposed to listen to me!

Ray (*laughing*)   Am I?

Laura   Yes! Look at you – far away in your own little world, dreaming your dreams.

Ray   I know, I –

Laura   The lights are on but there's nobody within miles!

Ray (*delighted laughter*)   That's right. Not even, not even squatters.

Laura   I'm serious.

Ray   Me too. Because . . . you are more screwy than me. Sometimes. You are. You're off your head. You've flipped your lid. You've popped your hatch . . .

She hits him with the pillow.

Laura   Shut up.

Ray   You've popped your cork, you're off your stick, you've lost your conkers, marbles . . .

She hits him with the pillow.

Laura   Shut up, you fool!

Ray (*laughing*)   You've burnt the soup. You've shredded the screw. You've lost the soap. You, you . . .

Laura   Come here.

He puckers his lips and moves his face closer. **Laura** *smacks him in the face.*

Ray (*delighted*)   Beautiful. Do it again.

She grabs him by the ears, makes to kiss him and blows a raspberry into his lips.

I like it. I really do, Laura. It blows me away.

Pause.

I just . . . I just want to put my body against your body. That's all I want. I like your body. I like the curves. I like the bumps and the . . . mounds. And what's inside. Whatever it is that . . . powers you, Laura, I like it. So warm. So warm.

Laura   Are you trying to tell me something?

Ray   I just did.

They look at each other. The phone rings.

Ray   Don't answer it. (*Beat.*) You don't like answering the phone, do you? Why not?

Ray *picks up the phone.* **Laura** *snatches it.*

Laura   Hello . . . hello?

Pause.

No thanks.

Pause.

Because I don't want to that's why. No . . . Because I don't. And I don't want to go to the pub . . . I don't want to play pool . . . I don't want to play darts either.

Pause.

No!

Ray   Hang up.

Laura   Don't you call me that.

Ray   Hang up the phone.

Laura   What? That's not a man's voice, I just coughed . . . So when I cough I sound like a man.

Ray *grabs at the phone.* **Laura** *hangs on and speaks into the phone.*

Laura   Bastard.

She slams the phone down. Pause.

He wants me to meet him. (*Beat.*) He says I have to meet him. (*Beat.*) He says if I don't meet him he's gonna break my legs.

Ray   What're you gonna do?

Laura   What do you think?

Pause. **Laura** *gets out of bed and pulls on jeans and a jumper.* **Ray** *gets up and searches for his clothes.*

Ray   He'll break your legs anyway. It doesn't make any difference to him. He's a/psychopath.

Laura   If I don't go and he comes round here he'll break your legs too!

Ray (*beat*)   You think so?

Laura   I know so.

He hesitates, then pulls on a pair of pants and pulls a jumper over his head and hops about with the pants half up and the jumper half on.

Ray   You need looking after. He needs dealing with. That's where I come into it.

Laura   Ray, no.

Ray   What if something happens?

Laura *goes to the bed, pulls from under the pillow a hammer. She picks up her bag, puts the hammer in the bag.*

Laura   Nothing is going to happen.

Ray What the fuck's that?

Laura What? This 'hammer'?

Ray Yeh.

Laura It's a hammer.

Ray You sleep with a hammer?

Laura I lost my baseball bat.

Ray I don't think that's wise, Laura. Nine times out of ten if you pull a hammer on somebody they'll use it on you. (*Beat.*) What if he tries to make friends with you or something? Tries to . . . worm his way back into your affections.

Laura Then it'd be a miracle.

They look at each other. **Laura** *exits.*

Scene Three

The river. **Dave** *and* **Laura** *sit on a bench by the water.* **Dave** *is wearing his suit, which is a little shabbier now, top button undone etc. He drinks from a bottle in a brown paper bag and is drunk.*

Dave I looked at myself in the mirror and I said to myself, I said, 'I am a man. A man who can look after his self but not a happy man. Not a complete man.' And then I asked myself, 'What is a man without a woman? What is he.' No job, no money, no faith will ever lead him to anything by his self. But with a woman . . .

Laura Isn't the sight of the empty bridge the most beautiful thing you ever seen?

Pause. **Dave** *drinks.*

Dave I was a miserable man, Laura. I saw the darkness stare me in the face. Sometimes I'd come over cloudy. All strangely cloudy and I'd ask myself, 'Why?' Why is the question. And then I'd put it to myself *hypothetically* what would we have done if we were married? And . . . and then I tell myself, 'We would've worked at it.'

Laura   But we weren't married.

Dave   Yes, but what if we were? And we did this to ourselves what we're doing now? Divorce? (*Singing vaguely.*)
D.I.V.O.R.C.E. King Henry the Eighth – he was not a happy man. Why? Because he didn't work at it. And why? Because . . . he had no son.

Laura   But we *weren't married*.

Dave   And why that? Because . . . because . . . I don't know why. I'm no philosopher, Laura, but thinking aside, you light my wick. Eh? You do it for me.

Long pause. He looks at her.

I don't want to be with another woman in the whole of Shepherd's Bush. I love you, Laura.

Laura   But that's what you say every time.

Dave   I mean it this time.

Laura   That's what you say every time too.

Dave   And I mean it every time.

Laura   Well, maybe you don't mean it enough.

Pause.

Dave   You know you say no to me, Laura, you say no to me every time but I know and you know, you mean *Yes*.

Laura   I have to go.

She makes a move to go, he puts a hand on her shoulder.

Dave   I'm trying to say I'm sorry.

Laura   You can't say you're sorry. There are things you can't apologise for, Dave. There are things you must not do and if you do 'em . . . then you can't apologise.

Dave   I never meant to hurt you.

Laura   Why did you?

Dave   I was under pressure . . .

Laura   *I* was under pressure!

Dave   There's a . . . force inside of me and I can't control it. I don't know what it is.

Laura   Thirteen pints of Guinness is most of it.

Dave   I'd do anything for you, Laura. I'd go on my knees for you. I'd do a ten stretch in the Scrubs, knock off Willy Hill's, blow up the Houses of fuckin' Parliament. I'm serious.

Pause.

I want to be a daddy.

Silence.

I said –

Laura   I heard.

Dave   But you –

Laura   I heard and I don't –

Dave   Can't comprehend.

Laura   No, I –

Dave   You're a bit surprised.

Laura   No, Dave –

Dave   You –

Laura   I don't believe my fuckin' ears is all.

Pause.

Dave   Think about it, Laura, eh? Will you do that?

Laura   He'll be born from the bottle but he won't be brought up by it.

Dave   I'll stop tomorrow.

Laura   You can't stop tomorrow.

Dave   I'm trying to do what's right.

Laura   You don't know what's right.

Dave And bringing a helpless kiddie into the world to live off slops and benefits is?

Laura We'll survive.

Dave What are you going to tell him when he wants his da'? When he wants a father's hand to hold in the night?

Laura It's not about that.

Dave It's about blood, Laura. Our blood and his blood. You know that's all that matters.

He produces a ring from his pocket, holds it up.

I found this. You didn't lose it, Laura . . . I did.

Pause. **Laura** *regards him. He holds it out to her insistently but she refuses to touch it.*

Laura You mean you lied.

Dave We could be a real family, Laura.

Laura Just leave me alone. I curse the day I met you.

Laura *gets up and walks away.*

Dave And the day I met you was the day the Angel of Joy came down from the heavens, so it was.

Dave *drinks.*

Scene Four

Pete's *flat.* **Pete**, **Ray** *and* **Laura** *are at the table, the remains of lunch, a few cans and a couple of bottles of wine spread in front of* **Ray**.

Ray Just lying around. Sleeping, eating, shopping. All the simple/things.

Laura Shopping? Don't talk to me about shopping. I've never seen anybody so afraid of a supermarket in my/life.

Ray Drinking, shagging –

Laura He's allergic to it, I think.

Ray   It's not the supermarket, Laura, it's the people. All those people bickering over which brand to buy, whether to buy meat or fish, is it cheaper in the market?

Laura   Everybody has to eat – tell him he has to eat, Pete.

Pete   You have to eat, Ray.

Ray   Haven't they got anything better to do except drag their fat arses around with their fat husbands and their screeching kids? If I was a mother I'd leave 'em there – let 'em gorge themselves to death on fucking Mars Bars.

Laura   He's banned shopping entirely.

Ray   There's a lot of things I've banned entirely.

Laura   Won't be seen dead on a bus.

Pete   I hate buses. People on buses are fools.

Laura   Tubes . . .

Ray   Why there's not more homicides on the tube I can't understand.

Laura   Completely anti-social. I thought/I was.

Ray   I just mind my own business, Laura.

Laura   You do not mind your own business. You don't.

Ray   I need a drink.

Ray *reaches for a bottle and refills his glass. Drinks.*

Pete   I think you've had enough.

Ray   Enough? No, that's just where you're wrong, Pete old boy – I haven't had nearly enough.

Pete   Come on, Ray. You've had your fun.

Pete *pulls the phial of pills from his pocket. Puts it on the table.* **Ray** *looks at it. Pause.*

Ray   I haven't even started yet.

Pete   I won't take no for an answer.

Ray That's the only reason you invited me, isn't it? You didn't want to meet her at all. You just got me round here to take me fuckin' dose.

Pete Now don't make a scene.

Ray 'Don't make a' . . . a what? Listen to his Lordship. I am sorry, Peter old fruit –

Pete Ray, come on.

Ray For getting in . . . for getting on your nerves and ruining your special . . . lunch time thingie. (*He laughs.*)

Pause.

Laura What are they?

Ray I have heart trouble.

Pete They're just pills he's taking.

Laura What're they for?

Pete They're just –

Ray They're to stop me getting upset when my big fucking/ bastard brother –

Pete Didn't he –

Ray Get's on my big . . . fucking . . . on my tits that's what they're for.

Pause.

Pete Didn't you . . . tell her about . . .

Ray About what, Pete?

Pete About . . .

Ray Oh, about '. . .'

Pete Yeh.

Ray No.

Pause.

Pete   Ray has to take this medication this special medication because sometimes he gets depressed.

Ray   I get depressed.

Pete   Doesn't sleep too well sometimes.

Ray   Can't sleep that's true.

Pete   Sometimes he *only* sleeps.

Ray   I do stupid things.

Pete   Yes he, stupid things, he –

Ray   I –

Pete   He –

Ray   I mean really stupid. Schizo.

Pete   Yeh he . . . schizo. (*Beat.*) That's what he does.

Pause.

Laura   Oh.

Ray   I mean I don't eat babies or anything like that.

Pete   No no no no no. No, he doesn't do that.

Silence.

(*To* **Laura**.) So when's it due?

Laura   What?

Pete   The . . .

Laura   Oh, the . . . December. Yeh December.

Pete   December.

Laura   December, yes.

Pete   Just in time for Christmas.

Ray   Now we're talking about babies.

Pete   Is it kicking yet?

Laura   No –

Ray   Now we're – if he kicks you –

Pete   Ray, that's/enough.

Ray   Kick him back. Give yourself a . . . do it yourself abortion. Save yourself the agony.

Pause.

Pete   Oh, Jesus.

Ray   I mean it. You should see the father.

Laura   I beg your pardon?

Ray   Christ knows what's gonna hatch.

Laura *smacks him in the face and stands.*

Pete   No, Laura, please.

Laura   That's the most horrible thing you could say to me. That's the most . . . that . . .

Ray   What?

Pete   Jesus, Ray, can't you –

Laura   Don't you get it? Don't you understand anything? I want this baby, Ray. I want it. I'm worried about it and I know I probably can't look after it properly but I want it. More than, more than anything . . .

She sits down. Pause.

Ray   I don't know why.

Pete   Ray –

Laura   Because it would be mine . . . mine forever and it wouldn't hurt me and it wouldn't upset me and it would love me and it would trust me and I would . . . I would trust . . . it . . .

Ray   But babies are horrible, Laura. They stink and cry and piss and poo everywhere. Everybody knows that.

Pete   Ray, for Christsake!

Laura *gets up and starts clearing plates.*

Pete   It's all right I'll do that.

Laura *ignores him.*

Pete   Talk sense, Ray, if you can.

Ray   I'm trying, Pete, I'm honestly trying to.

Pete   Shh . . . just don't say another word. You push people too far.

Laura   It's all right, Pete, I'm sorry.

Ray   No, Pete, no I don't because you push me too far. You two . . . you don't even know each other. What the fuck do you care about each other? You pretend that's all . . . you pretend to care that she . . . you pretend to have this concern that I . . . you're just . . . You know what you are? You're . . . selfish. And . . . responsible. Incredibly responsible.

Pause. To **Laura**.

Not you, him.

Laura   I think we should be going.

Ray   I'm going to piss.

Ray *gets up,* **Laura** *stops him.*

Laura   Come now if you're coming. You can piss at my place. (*To* **Pete**.) Thanks for the –

Pete   Any time –

Ray   Why would I wanna piss at your place? Sit around at your place waiting for Joe Bugner to come home and –

Laura   That's enough!

Ray   Give us both another beating?

Laura   I'll give you a beating if you/don't –

Ray   Cos that's what's gonna happen. Oh yes, I can tell, he's gonna come around and he's gonna kill us both dead in our bed. And then I am going to kill him and then they'll put me away for good. They'll never let me go cos I'll be in Broadmoor or something with Jack The Fucking Yorkshire Ripper do you want that do you think that's reasonable? Eh? Well, do you?

Laura *just looks at him, can't speak. She grabs her bag and exits. Long pause.*

Ray   She's got a hammer in that bag. She has. She's more barmy than me.

Pete   Are you gonna tell me what that was about?

Ray   No.

Pause.

Pete   Why did you do that? Why do you have to . . . (*He breaks off. Pause.*)

Ray   I'm drunk, Pete.

Pete   Well, why do you have to drink like that?

Ray   I get depressed.

Pete   But, Ray, you drink when you're depressed, you drink when you're happy, when you're bored, it doesn't help.

Ray   It does.

Pete   She's having a baby, man. There's some fella out there who's having a baby *with* her. I mean a married woman's one thing but up the spout's a whole new kettle of fish, Ray.

Ray   She's not married.

Pete   Does she want to be?

Ray   She just –

Pete   How well do you know her? How well does she know you? Have you even considered –

Ray   No I haven't considered.

Pete   The implications? (*Beat.*) I mean I'm coming to the end of my rope here. I'm right at the end. This is just . . . you're just . . . this is just hanging on a hair here. I can't fucking do it any more.

Ray (*beat*)   Well, that's life, isn't it?

Pete   I mean . . . 'Selfish'? 'Responsible'?

Pause.

Maybe you're right. Maybe that's where I've gone wrong . . .
Maybe my wife left me because I was this selfish cunt who wore
a pinny and tossed salads all day for other people. Maybe I
should never have tried to save dad or his greasy old caff or his
doomed fuckin' life cos that would have just been responsible, I
dunno . . .

Ray   You bought him out, Pete. It was the one thing he loved
and you took it off of him for a handful of notes.

Pete   Jesus, Ray – I just . . . had this weird idea that the thing
to do was to go to work and do an honest day and pay a few bills
and look after your family and . . . I mean . . . he couldn't do it.
I mean sooner or later somebody's gotta . . . make a stand. I
don't see what's wrong with that.

Pause.

Ray   Well, it's a bit boring, innit, Pete . . .

Pete   You're not the only one going out of your mind. You
know I'd jack this in tomorrow if I had half a chance. Get on the
old rock'n'roll and piss off to the seaside with some little bird I
met in the pub . . . I'd love to.

Ray   Why don't you?

Pete   Because I am obliged, Ray . . . to do this thing for you.
It is what I have to do. You understand? The measure of a man
(no, listen to me) in this life is whether he can do . . . what he
thinks he has to do.

Pause.

I mean . . . why do you say these things to people?

Ray   I don't know.

Pete   Is it you or is it the . . . sooner or later you're gonna have
to make up your mind. (*Beat.*) Tell me. (*Beat.*) Please.

Ray (*suddenly laughing*)   You're breaking my heart.

Pete   *What?*

Ray   Who fucking cares?

Ray *continues to laugh and swigs on a bottle.*

Pete   Get out.

Ray   What?

Pete   It's none of my business. It isn't and I cannot make it my business no matter who says I should. I have my own business.

Ray *gets up and starts to go.*

Pete   I mean it I've had enough. You just –

Ray   OK.

Pete   Get.

Ray *exits.*

Scene Five

Wasteland. **Ives** *stands alone.* **Ray** *is huddled under old blankets, paper and his coat at the foot of a nearby wall.*

Ives   There will be a zone for the lost and the loveless and the Godless and the demented and the dead and the half dead and the damned and all of those who no longer live in the light, who only live in the dark. And that zone will be a terrifying place, and that zone will be the only place, and that zone will be all around you. You will not be able to walk in the streets that you walked in tonight. You will not be able to go where you are going without seeing the zone, or some small part of it, or one of the beasts that live in the zone, or the beast that made the zone. Believe me. There is nowhere. Nowhere you can go to hide from it. Nothing you can do to eradicate it. You will never be able to clean it. You will never sweep it under the rug. The city will become that zone. You will all be of that zone. The zone that is the turd that you can never polish. You are all flies. Flies on the fleck of shit that is this world.

Ray   Ives . . .

Ives   Your world. The new world. Your new home. It will be built by contractors and its management put out to tender.

There will be no crèche, no fire escape, no stairs and it will stink of piss and disease just like every other place before it.

Ray   I'm trying to sleep.

Ives   Don't deny it. You can't argue with me. You can't tell me, you don't believe me, when I tell you, that you are going to burn in hell. I am going to burn in hell, the blossoms on the trees are going to burn in hell.

Ray   Have you made any money yet?

Ives   I know what I am talking about. I am the authority on this kind of thing. I am the only authority you want to listen to and if you don't believe me you can jam it up your arses and whistle because I have had enough. I am disgusted with you, with me, with everything and I am tired of telling you.

Ray *gets to his feet and puts his hands over his ears.*

Ray   Shut up, I'm not listening.

Ives   I am disgusted with the sky. With the water. The trees bore the daylights out of me . . .

Ray   No, stop!

Ives *staggers and collapses.*

Ives   I know you don't like it. I don't like it. But I told you this would happen. I warned you. I'm trying to be reasonable about it . . .

Silence.

Ray   Ives . . . Ives old boy. Don't die on me now.

Ives   Nightmares . . . nightmares happen . . .

Ray   Come on, Ives . . . we'll go somewhere warm. I'll take you to a launderette.

Ives   I brought home the bacon once . . . I did . . . to my wife.

Pause.

From the Isle of Skye, she was.

He's dead. **Ray** *just stares at him, unable to shift his gaze. He looks around suddenly, distracted by a noise.*

Ray   What d'you mean?

Pause.

What's wrong with the launderette? He was cold.

Pause.

No, because there's nothing wrong with me.

Ray *stares straight ahead, listening.*

Scene Six

Laura's *bedsit. Early morning.* **Laura**, *dressed in leggings and a sweater, is sitting on the end of the bed, staring into space. There is a knock at the door.* **Laura** *doesn't move. Another knock and she goes to it.*

Laura   Who is it?

Ray (*offstage*)   It's me.

Laura *hesitates then goes to the door, thinks better of it and backs up, nervous.*

Ray   Laura?

Pause. Another knock.

Are you all right?

Laura   What do you want?

Ray   I want to come in.

Laura   It's seven o'clock in the morning.

Ray   I have to talk to you. I have something to tell you.

Laura   What is it, Ray?

Ray   Let me in and I'll tell you.

She opens the door a crack.

I missed you.

Laura   Ray, you have to go.

Ray   Did you miss me?

Laura   Not really, no.

Ray   I was worried about you.

Laura   Were you now.

Ray   Yes. I can't stop thinking about you. I keep thinking about when we were in the field in the countryside. The grass was like hay and the yellow sun shone and shone . . . we were making hay while the sun shone, weren't we, Laura?

Laura   Yeh, that's right –

He brushes past into the room.

Ray   We were making hay while the sun shone, weren't we?

Laura   What do you want?

Ray   But it was more than that, wasn't it?

Laura   Ray, I'm begging you –

Ray   It was more than that.

Laura   I'm not well.

Ray   What's wrong with you? Are you sick?

Laura   I'm just tired.

Ray   How sick?

Laura   It's too late.

Ray   You looked so beautiful . . .

Laura   Keep away.

Ray   We kissed and you smelt of blossom.

Dave *enters in trousers but no shirt, a towel slung over his shoulder. Stands at the door unseen by* **Ray**.

Ray   You understand me, Laura.

Laura   No I don't! Shut up!

Ray   Yes you do and I understand you and there is nothing else. There is nothing else is there Laura? Nothing that matters . . . I know I'm in trouble now. I can tell things are going wrong – but I just . . . I, I, I, I love you, Laura.

Dave *laughs.* **Ray** *glances over his shoulder and sees* **Dave**. *Turns around to face him. Pause.*

Dave (*mimicking*)   'I, I, l-l-love you Laura.' (*Beat.*) You gonna introduce us?

Pause.

Laura (*to* **Ray**)   I'll be seeing you.

Dave   Fine way to speak to a lady. Is everything all right then, Laura?

Laura   It's fine.

Dave   Who's yer man then?

Laura   Nobody.

Dave   I'll tell you what, he looks familiar.

Laura   He's going.

Dave *scrutinises* **Ray**.

Dave   Maybe it's the pub. You drink in the Adelaide there? I seen a few fellows like you in the Adelaide. Queer fellows. D'you think that's where our paths crossed? Doesn't say much, does he?

Laura   Ray . . .

Dave   He's got a name then. Nice name. Are you gonna tell me what's going on?

Laura   He's going, Dave.

Dave   Are you gonna tell me what's going on or not?

Ray   Leave, leave her alone please.

Dave (*mimicking*)   'L-leave her alone please. L-leave her a-l-one p-please.' (*Laughs.*) He can talk then yer man? Not very well but it's a start.

Laura   Ray, go.

Ray   What . . . what have you done?

Laura   Nothing, just –

Ray   What have you done!

Laura   I don't know I can't tell you!

Ray *just stares at her then tries to leave,* **Dave** *bars his way.*

Dave   No no no no no no no. No no no no no no no. Oh no. I don't think you should do that. I mean you can if you want – if you're the type of man who does something just because his lady friend gets her keks in a twist –

Laura   Don't start, Dave.

Ray   Get, get out my way please.

Dave   I beg your pardon?

Ray   Get out my way thank you. Please I would like you to get out my –

Dave   *SHE* LOVES *ME* – YOU UNDERSTAND? SHE. LOVES ME.

Laura   I don't, I don't!

Dave   Cunt. Shut up!

Laura   Please!

Dave   ON YOUR KNEES! (*To* **Ray**.) What are you looking at?

He grabs **Ray** *by the shirt, backs him up a few paces very fast against the bed and flings him across it,* **Ray** *lands on the floor beside the bed.*

Dave (*to* **Laura**)   Knees!

Laura, *panicked, gets on her knees.*

Dave (*to* **Ray**)   Watch.

Laura   No . . . no . . . no . . .

Dave *undoes his belt, gets behind* **Laura** *and ties her hands behind her back.* **Ray** *watches horrified. He wrestles with the belt, pushes* **Laura**'s *head down roughly,* **Laura** *struggles.*

Dave   Why him, Laura? Eh?

Laura (*struggling*)   Why not him?

Dave *pulls* **Laura**'s *leggings down, tying up her legs.*

Dave   Cos he's a fucking eejit that's why. I've seen him, mincing about like a fairy with his brother, talking to his self, I've seen him, everybody has. Mad as a fucking whippet. (*To* **Ray**.) I know you. I know who you are. Did you think I didn't recognise you?

Laura   Please –

Dave   I warned you. Did I not say I'd kill you?

Laura *struggles and they move a semicircle. He pulls the belt tight with several jerks. Concentrating, his back to* **Ray**. **Ray** *reaches under the pillow, withdraws the hammer, walks over to* **Dave** *and hits him twice with the hammer.* **Dave** *instantly collapses and* **Laura** *struggles out from under.*

Laura   No! Christ no!

Ray   Evil fucker. You're *evil*!

Ray *hovers,* **Laura** *wrestles the hammer away.*

Laura   Ray!

Ray   Burn in hell. Yes, you. *Hell.*

Pause. **Ray** *looks at* **Laura** *then runs out.* **Laura** *stands there in shock.*

Laura   Oh, Jesus . . . Jesus Mary and Joseph.

She catches her breath then kneels down beside **Dave**, *tries to turn him over but can't. Suddenly he stirs, she jumps to her feet.*

I'll . . . call an ambulance.

Dave *struggles to get up,* **Laura** *picks up the hammer and fidgets with it watching* **Dave** *and dialling the telephone. He collapses again and tries to heave himself up.* **Laura** *drops the phone and watches* **Dave**.

Laura   Stay where you are, Dave . . . I'm warning you . . .

Scene Seven

Hospital. **Laura** *and* **Pete** *sit on chairs in casualty.* **Pete** *smokes a cigarette.*

Pete   I went in there. I went and saw this woman he's been seeing. Turns out he hasn't been seeing her – what am I talking about – I knew he hadn't been seeing her. They never even heard of him. I say, 'How come you never heard of him?' They say, 'Because he didn't fill out the form.' 'What are you talking about?' I say. 'I filled out the form.' 'No, you filled out *your* form,' they say. 'He's supposed to fill out his form and take it to a different building.' 'I filled out the fucking form,' I say. 'I did everything to the letter.' 'No,' they say, 'you filled out the form to say he filled out his form. If he didn't fill out his form then it's null and void.' (*Beat.*) Then they gave me more forms. Emergency forms or something. Review forms. They say it isn't too late for him to fill it in now, if he fills it in now and brings it back Monday they could help. If I can find him and be so good as to get a pen in his hand. What am I, a fucking magician? Where are these people who make the rules? Where are they hiding – can't they see what's happening? (*Beat.*) The man's lying in there with his brain stoved in. What are we gonna say? He . . . beat himself to death? Just for the hell of it? He could've died . . . We should tell somebody. Maybe we could explain.

Laura   Explaining never got anyone anywhere. We'll explain he fell out of bed.

Pete   Laura –

Laura   And down a flight of stairs. You'd be surprised what can happen to a person falling out of bed.

Pete   He'll tell them!

Laura   He's a fucking vegetable – how's he going to tell 'em?

Pete   If he comes round –

Laura   He won't.

Pause.

Pete   How do you know? He got a few whacks in the head a cracked skull they'll do this emergency operation and bob's your uncle.

Laura   He got more than a few.

Pete   What d'you mean?

Pause.

Laura   He was trying to get up.

Pete   When?

Laura   Later, later he tried to get up so I . . . gave him a couple more is all. Just a tap. Here and there.

Pause.

Pete   What are you telling me, Laura?

Laura   I –

Pete   That between the two of you you just hammered this man half to death? That you and him just took it in turns . . . hammering your boyfriend to . . .

Laura   He just tried to kill me. What's he gonna tell them?

Pete   I feel sick.

Laura   Don't be such a baby.

Pete   No I do, I really . . . I'm surrounded by maniacs.

Long pause.

I should go and . . .

Laura   Yes you go and . . .

Pete   If I know Ray he's probably in the pub. What d'you think? That wouldn't surprise me.

Laura   He won't be in the pub.

Pete   How do you know?

Laura   Face it, Pete!

Pause. **Pete** *gets up.*

Pete   Will you be all right . . . I mean . . . on your own?

Pause.

Laura   I want to be on my own.

Pete *exits. Lights down slowly on* **Laura**.

Scene Eight

Restaurant kitchen. **Ray** *is wearing* **Pete**'*s whites and chef's hat. He holds a rusty old petrol can and walks in a circle around the kitchen, carefully pouring. He finishes and sets the can down. Pats his pockets.* **Pete** *appears at the door silently, looking haggard and wearing* **Ray**'*s old long coat.* **Ray** *doesn't notice him for a moment and* **Pete** *hasn't yet noticed the petrol.*

Ray   You got a light?

Pete   What do you want a light for?

Ray   I got a few things here I want to set fire to.

Pete   What things?

Ray   Everything.

Pete *comes into the kitchen, sniffs with growing alarm, looks at* **Ray** *who produces a lighter and holds it up.* **Pete** *stops.*

Pete   JESUS WHAT ARE YOU DOING?

Ray   This is where it all happens, isn't it, Pete?

Pete   This . . . yes is where I work, Ray, you can't –

Ray   Yes and where dad worked before you and I worked with him.

Pete   That's right, Ray –

Ray   In this kitchen here.

Pete   Yes.

Ray   Which is in this restaurant.

Pete   Yes, my restaurant! Everything/I own.

Ray   Which is in this family.

Pete   Yes, it's in the family!

Ray   I don't like families.

Pete   Well, they're all different/aren't they?

Ray   I wasn't good enough at doing the dishes so they sent me away.

Pete   No, Ray –

Ray   And I got sick because I wasn't strong enough.

Pete   You were sick because you were sick/there's no –

Ray   And then dad killed mum.

Pete (*beat*)   *What?*

Ray   It's true. He left her and then she died.

Pete   It was breast cancer.

Ray   She died because she wasn't strong enough.

Pete   She was very ill, sometimes that happens . . .

Ray   Dad wasn't strong enough either, was he?

Pete (*desperate*)   I don't know what you're talking about!

Ray   None of us was strong enough.

Pete   Ray, please!

Ray   None of us! This fuckin' family . . . it's cursed . . . marked!

Pete   Give me the lighter!

Ray   Damned.

Ray *catches his breath and hands* **Pete** *the lighter, as* **Pete** *takes it* **Ray** *whips another from his pocket and holds it up.*

Pete   Jesus!

Ray   But you can cook, can't you, Pete?

Pete   Yes.

Ray   So let's cook! Uh?

He upends the petrol can over his head, **Pete** *covers his eyes in anguish.*

Pete   NO!

Ray   Cook everything and make it worthwhile! Make it something that people want.

Pete   . . . You can't . . .

Ray   And need.

Pete   Please, I'm . . . begging you.

Ray *hands him the lighter quickly,* **Pete** *takes it and* **Ray** *withdraws another from his pocket.*

Ray   You know what I think, Pete?

Pete   I have no idea.

Ray   I think I wasted my life. What are the chances of me getting a job in this gaff?

Pete   Well, Ray . . . this is a very small operation. I don't employ that many/people.

Ray   Yes but you could employ me! I'm your brother.

Pete   It doesn't work like that any more. It wouldn't help. What would help is me running this place/successfully.

Ray   It would help me, you cunt!

Pete   I am helping you this is how I'm helping you!

Ray *tries to light the lighter.* **Pete** *makes a lunge at* **Ray** *and* **Ray** *dodges.*

Pete   Christ, no, no!

Ray   I can't stand it, Pete! I just can't stand it any more!

Pete *keeps his distance as* **Ray** *attempts to ignite the lighter, it won't light.*

Pete   Leave it alone!

He grabs hold of **Ray**. *They wrestle over the lighter and* **Pete** *gets it.*

STOP!

Ray   I can't stop – get off of me!

He breaks away, suddenly changing.

What?! Shut up! Shut . . . I'm not listening. Jesus, no!

Pete   You . . . you . . . talk to me for fuck's sake. Tell me what it is.

Ray *has his hands clamped over his ears and is watching* **Pete**. *Silence. They catch their breath.*

Pete   It's the . . . it's the voices, isn't it?

Ray *trembling, finally nods.*

Pete   They've come back. (**Ray** *nods.*) What are they saying?

Ray   They say . . . all different things.

Pete   Like what?

Pause.

Come on, Ray, you can tell me.

Pause. **Ray** *produces another lighter from his pocket.*

Please . . .

Ray   They say to me that I should . . . go somewhere and . . .

Pete   Go somewhere. Go where?

Ray   Go everywhere . . .

Pete   Everywhere OK . . .

Ray   And and find . . . something although I don't know what it is.

Pete   Well, like what?

Pause. **Pete** *reaches out for the lighter slowly,* **Ray** *draws away slowly.*

Ray   Find a way of stopping things happening.

Pete   What things?

Ray   Things like this obviously.

Pete   And?

Ray   Find a way of . . . living with . . . memory.

Pete   Memory yes . . .

Ray   Cos that's what triggers it I'm sure. Or else . . . signals from somewhere . . . possibly the saucepans and the metal objects transmit signals but I can't be sure.

Pete   I doubt it.

Ray   Yes, but if we set fire to everything then if there were any transmitters they'd be ruined wouldn't they?

Pete   Let's just concentrate on the memories.

Ray   OK . . .

Pete   What memories?

Ray (*beat*)   Like the time remember when we were kids . . . when things first started happening . . . and dad comes home and . . . it's hot, a hot summer and we're walking down Fulham Palace Road on the big wide pavement and we're talking and I turn to look at him . . . I just get a glimpse of him and . . . I just notice how filthy he is and unshaven and how he stinks and he wears . . . like an old blue safari suit . . . and there are little specs of blood round the collar where he cuts himself shaving . . . and his teeth, his eyes . . . his eyes are brown, all of it brown even the white bits are brown. And I think . . . I think . . . I'll be like that one day.

Pause.

(*Dazed. Listening.*) They scare the shit out of me. They say very fucking weird things I can tell you. Things even too weird for you to figure out, Pete. I try to get real people to talk to me so I can compare the difference but it's not easy.

Pause.

What do they say to you?

Pete   I don't get them, Ray.

Ray   Oh.

Silence.

Pete   But I know . . . I know dad had . . . a bit of difficulty with things. He had a sort of . . . faith . . . in things which ruined him.

Ray   I don't have any faith, Pete. (*Beat.*) Some people just don't.

Long pause. **Pete** *takes the lighter from* **Ray** *gently.*

What's going to happen to me?

Pete   Nothing.

Ray   Nothing? Ever?

Pete (*gently*)   What do you want to happen?

Ray   I don't want the injections.

Pete   Nobody's giving you injections.

Ray   My four-weekly injections. They'll give me them after four weeks, they're like that.

Pete *puts an arm round* **Ray** *to comfort him.*

Pete   Come on, it's OK.

Ray   I know it's OK but it doesn't seem OK and . . . have you got a fag?

Pete *shakes his head.*

Ray   I just thought I'd ask but I understand if you don't.

Pete *pats him on the shoulder, drapes a couple of dishcloths around him and carefully mops him dry as they speak.*

Ray   Because you don't smoke, do you, Pete?

Pete   Not normally no, no.

Ray I got the lighters in King Street. I know that fellow who sells them, you know. I know that fellow. Six for a pound.

Pete Bargain.

Ray In Shepherd's Bush Market there's a fellow who sells real guns. Imagine that.

Pete Real guns, really?

Ray Yes for twelve pounds ninety-nine which is a bit steep.

Pete For a real gun yes.

Ray And monkeys. Real monkeys or at least very big bags of peanuts.

Pete Well, that's wonderful.

Ray Yes. Real monkeys.

Pete *takes his coat off and helps* **Ray** *into it.*

Scene Nine

A kitchen in a hostel. **Ray** *and* **Pete** *are cooking on a portable hot plate.* **Pete** *chops and stirs etc. while* **Ray** *looks on vaguely, sedated.*

Pete I got it in the market. It's quite neat. It's compact, see, and it doesn't use much power so if you – if you do accidently set fire to anything you fling a blanket over it and the flames are contained. It's not much cop for fry-ups but if you want a plate of beans or a nice cup of warm milk to help you sleep it takes two minutes.

Ray I thought gas was better.

Pete It is better, but this is your own. Your own little cooker, you keep it in your room and you don't have to come out for anything.

Ray They got gas here. I've seen it. Big – big hob.

Pete Will they let you use it?

Ray Dunno.

He considers it and makes a face.

You think of everything, Pete –

Pete   Yes I do.

Ray   You're a clever man.

Pete   You're a clever man too.

He stirs a pan on the hot plate.

Now. Onions.

Ray   Onions.

Pete   Always fry 'em in butter.

Ray   Yes.

Pete   Tastes better, gives it a better consistency. You come down and the pan's all dirty (cos all this stuff's dirty) and you use margarine it'll go black and thin. Butter stays thick.

Ray   Got it.

Pete   Especially for soup.

Ray   Soup, right.

Pete   They get the tinned soups in here every week but if you wanna make your own or you wanna make a sauce, a nice pasta dish, you use butter or oil and the fats from the thing. From what you're cooking. Have a whiff.

Ray *sniffs at the pan.*

Ray   Nice. What about eggs?

Pete   Fried eggs?

Ray   No, omelette.

Pete   In this instance yes we use butter.

Ray   Because it's better.

Pete   In this instance yes but just for an egg normally that can be expensive. (*Beat.*) Eggs aren't important. Eggs are eggs.

Ray   Everybody here likes fried eggs.

Pete   I don't often cook eggs. If I do, I don't fry 'em anyway. If I did, I wouldn't use butter. Just my preference.

Ray   Cos you're a businessman.

Pete   I'm a businessman, that's right.

Pause.

Ray   Laura used to use butter.

Pete   Laura's not a businessman.

Ray   No and she's not a business woman either. She just used to cook sometimes.

Pete   That's different. If you cook for a friend then you go that extra mile. If you ever have any friends over to this place I'll bring you some butter.

Ray   Thank you.

Pete   My pleasure.

He cooks.

Now. Always put your onions in long before any garlic. Garlic burns too quick and you can fuck it up.

Ray   Onions beforehand.

Pete   That's right.

Ray   Long long before.

Pete   That's right.

Ray   How long before?

Pete   Till they go translucent.

Ray   It's . . . an art, isn't it?

Pete   It's a very creative thing and it keeps your mind occupied. Feeding people is a serious business. Never use tinned tomatoes. Too watery and acidic. Use 'em fresh and always put 'em in last, very last so they don't disintegrate.

Ray   Disintegrate, yeh.

Pause.

Laura used to use tinned.

Pete   Well, it's not advisable.

Ray   It's cheaper. One time I saw them for twenty-three pee a tin. Tesco's.

Pete   Money isn't everything.

Ray   But twenty-three pee a tin, Pete . . .

Pete   What d'you wanna put in now?

Pause.

Ray   Did . . . did you speak to her then?

Pete   Yes I did. What do you want – mushroom?

Ray   Eggs.

Pete   We're not ready for eggs yet. Eggs come last.

Ray   Mushroom then.

Pete   Mushroom. Now we are talking.

Pete *puts the mushrooms in.*

Ray   What did she say? More mushrooms – what did she say?

Pete (*beat*)   Well . . . it's not really very good news, Ray.

Ray   Mm-hm.

Pete   She's had a lot to cope with.

Ray   Mm-hm.

Pete   She says she wants to try and . . . get herself together for a while. Get her life back together, for the kid maybe.

Ray   Can we put the eggs in now?

Pete   Not yet. (*Beat.*) She said she's actually quite happy on her own. She doesn't really want to . . . threaten that.

Ray *nods. Pause.*

Pete   She . . . she doesn't really want to see you again. For a while.

Pause.

Ray   Not till she's feeling better.

Pete   No.

Ray   And . . . and not till I'm feeling a bit better perhaps.

Pete   Not for a while.

Ray   Not for a long while no. How long?

Pete   She didn't say. I mean you can't really say, can you?

Pause.

Ray   Roughly.

Pete   She said she didn't know.

Ray   What, she didn't have any idea at all?

Pete   I think maybe she might try and go home or something.

Ray   She won't go home.

Pete   She said maybe she might write to you . . . in a few months.

Ray   How many months, six?

Pete   Six, maybe six, yes.

Ray   Six, OK. Six.

Pause.

Six months exactly or less?

Pete   It's just a guess, Ray. It could be less, could be a bit more . . . When she's had the kid maybe.

Ray   Right.

Pause.

Pete   I mean she's a nice girl Laura, but you . . . you gotta remember she's got her own life to lead. And she did before you came on the scene and before the other guy and she'll do what she can to keep that life on track. It's the way people are.

Ray   Because . . . we had a good time together. We understood each other.

Pete   I know but also you have your own life to lead too. You gotta think about yourself now. What you're gonna do with yourself.

Ray   I don't really want to think about that.

Pete   Well, it happens to the best of us. Sooner or later we're all on our own for a while. And then we're with someone again. And then we're alone again maybe. Swings and roundabouts.

Pause.

Ray   She's very very beautiful, Pete. Did you notice that? I don't think I've ever met anybody as beautiful as that. I mean . . . seriously, she's the type of girl you'd die for. People say they'd die for this person or for that person but I mean this time round I found out . . . what they meant. She's the type you could hold in your arms and gaze at without even . . . getting squeamish or anything. You could . . . you could say you loved her and have absolutely no regrets about it that's for sure. (*Beat.*) You'd love her all over, everything about her. Her face, her legs, her arms, her shoulders, her feet, her toes, breasts, hair, hands. (*Beat.*) Knees. Neck. Her laugh, she had a blindin' laugh, Pete, which was because of her eyes, she had very dark blue twinkling eyes. (*Beat.*) Her mouth. Her lips, lips like a duck's which – like this – which shows she's thoughtful, doesn't it, Pete?

Pete   Well . . . I'm sure she's thinking about you, Ray. I'm sure you'll never stop thinking about each other.

Ray   No.

Pete   No.

Long pause. **Pete** *picks up a clump of basil and sniffs it, then hands it to* **Ray** *who also sniffs it.*

When you chop the basil, always use more than you think you'll need. It grows on trees so use it like it grows on trees. Be generous with it. (*Beat.* **Ray** *nods.*) You have a go.

Ray *takes the knife and chops the basil carefully.* **Pete** *watches as he sprinkles it into the pan. Lights down slowly.*

Blackout.

Pale Horse

for Sarah Ward

'I looked, and behold a pale horse: and his name that sat on him was Death, and Hell followed with him.' (Revelation: *6, 8)*

Pale Horse was first performed at the Royal Court Theatre Upstairs, London, on 12 October 1995. The cast was as follows:

Charles	Ray Winstone
Lucy	Kacey Ainsworth
Undertaker	Terence Beesley
Vicar	Howard Ward
GP	Lynne Verrall
Maître d'	Howard Ward
Woman in Cemetery	Lynne Verrall
Woman Drinker	Lynne Verrall
Drinker One	Terence Beesley
Drinker Two	Howard Ward
Police Constable	Terence Beesley
Woman Police Constable	Lynne Verrall

Directed by Ian Rickson
Designed by Kandis Cook
Lighting by Johanna Town
Sound by Paul Arditti

Characters

Charles
Lucy
Undertaker
Vicar
GP
Maître d'
Woman in Cemetery
Woman Drinker
Drinker One
Drinker Two
Police Constable
Woman Police Constable

The action takes place over a period of about four weeks at various locations around south London.

Act One

Scene One

Bar.

Charles *is speaking on a wall phone and holding an unopened bottle of rum.*

Charles   I know. I know. I know. I know.

Pause.

I didn't know that.

Pause.

I didn't know that either.

Pause.

Because I believe in giving people a chance.

Pause.

No. I sacked him.

Pause.

Because he was a wanker. The point is I've now got six cases of Navy rum on my doorstep and no staff.

Pause.

Six bottles I asked for.

Pause.

Captain Morgan.

Pause.

I'm not selling it on – it's not a chain letter.

Pause.

Who's going to buy six cases of Navy rum? It's evil-looking.

Pause.

She's OK. The very oxygen I breathe.

Pause.

No, she can't stand the place. Thinks it's a 'den of iniquity'.

Pause.

How can it be a den of iniquity? Nobody comes here.

Pause.

I gotta go. Ta ta. Yeah, ta ta.

He hangs up and it rings immediately. He lifts the receiver and hangs up. It rings again. He answers.

Hello.

Pause.

That's me.

Pause.

What about her?

Pause.

When? Where? No, I didn't know . . .

Pause.

I'll come down.

He hangs up and stares straight ahead.

Scene Two

Funeral parlour.

Charles and an **Undertaker** *stand either side of a body in a bag on a slab.*

Charles You've done a good job.

Slight pause.

It's very lifelike.

Undertaker   I haven't done it yet.

Charles   Oh.

Pause.

Undertaker   I've done the preliminaries but embalming is a laborious, very specialised process.

Charles   Why's that?

Undertaker   Eh?

Charles   What makes it so specialised?

Slight pause.

Undertaker   I don't discuss the embalming process with relatives.

Charles   No, go on. What happens first?

Undertaker   I can't discuss it.

Charles   I'm curious. I might find it . . . therapeutic.

Undertaker   I drain all the blood out and I replace it with formaldehyde to preserve the flesh. I suck the blood out with this piece of apparatus here and pump in the embalming fluid with this one here.

He holds up a piece of apparatus.

The blood goes in a big white bucket and when I've finished it goes down the drain.

Charles   You can't reuse it? For a transfusion or something?

Undertaker   Can't reuse it, more's the pity.

Charles   Not even if she left herself to science?

*Slight pause. The **Undertaker** checks a clipboard.*

Undertaker   How do you mean?

Charles   Would you have to save it?

Undertaker   Did she or didn't she?

Charles No. But hypothetically, if that happened, would you have to hang on to the blood?

Undertaker They keep it at the hospital.

Charles Oh.

The **Undertaker** *looks at him.*

Pause.

Charles I'm making conversation. At times like this it's recommended you make conversation.

Slight pause.

Because it's science, isn't it? And science isn't . . . emotional.

Slight pause.

It's unemotional.

Slight pause.

Like the weather. What's the worse job you've ever done?

Undertaker I don't talk about that stuff.

Charles No, you're all right, I'm interested.

Pause.

Undertaker Suicides.

Charles Suicides, really?

Undertaker Found a young woman last week by the tracks at Southfields. Head completely severed. Body remained undiscovered for weeks. Picked her up, entrails gushed out in a puddle at my feet.

Charles No.

Undertaker Little children larking about, bringing their dogs along. I ask myself, Why? Week in, week out, dealing with the mutilated and the rotted and the dead. It's very sad.

Pause.

You want to know which type of people kill themselves the most?

Charles   Which?

Undertaker   People with families.

Charles   Right.

Undertaker   And people without families. Lonely people. Single people.

Charles   Single people?

Undertaker   Sometimes one goes and another follows. Sometimes it's like dominoes and the whole lot go. It's what life does to us. It kills us.

Silence.

Charles   Any money in it?

Undertaker   You reap what you sow.

Silence.

Any thoughts on a coffin?

Charles   I don't want anything flash. Bit skint at the moment.

Undertaker   Well, there's a nice teak just come in that's a bit special. Brass handles, silk lining and a kind of domed top with an arched support. It's nice.

Charles *gazes at the corpse.*

Undertaker   It's very discreet. I'll show you a catalogue. When do you fancy the funeral?

Slight pause.

Mr Strong?

Charles   As soon as possible. A weekday.

Undertaker   Weekdays are booked out until the weekend I'm afraid. Less traffic on the roads. I could do a Monday, only not this Monday.

Charles   Whenever.

Undertaker   I can do a weekend only, again, you've left it a bit late for this weekend.

Charles Just do what you have to do.

He gently reaches into the bag and strokes the face of the corpse.

Could I say goodbye?

Undertaker Be my guest.

Charles *leans down to kiss the corpse.*

Undertaker Hey, don't kiss it.

Charles Why not?

Undertaker It's unhygienic. More than my job's worth.

Charles Oh . . . sorry.

The **Undertaker** *goes.*

Scene Three

Cemetery.

A **Vicar** *and* **Charles** *stand by a grave. The* **Vicar** *scatters dust into the grave.*

Vicar '. . . Then shalt the dust return to the earth as it was: and the spirit shall return unto God who gave it.' Amen. Now let us turn our attention to Charles, to whom I give this counsel in his loss: 'Have ye not read in the Book of Moses, how in the bush God spake unto him, saying I am the God of Abraham, and the God of Isaac, and the God of Jacob?

Slight pause.

He is not the God of the dead, but the God of the living.'

Charles No. I haven't read that.

Slight pause.

So. What now?

Vicar The grave is filled in and you go home.

Charles I meant, what should I do now?

Vicar   You don't do anything. The gravediggers do all that.

Charles   Should I say some more prayers or something?

Vicar   Would you like to?

Charles   Which ones?

Vicar   Any ones you like.

Charles   I don't know any.

Vicar   Perhaps you have a prayer of your own.

Charles   Make one up, you mean?

Vicar   Yes.

Charles   Something about her. Personal.

Vicar   Absolutely.

Charles   About, you know, how lovely she was, stuff like that?

Vicar   'Whatsoever things are true, whatsoever things are just, whatsoever things are pure, whatsoever things are lovely . . . if there be any virtue, if there be any praise, think on these things.' Philippians, chapter four, verse eight.

Charles   Right.

Vicar   Have you read the Bible?

Charles   No, as it happens. Never had cause to.

Vicar   Was it not read to you as a child?

Charles   Family of agnostics.

Vicar   Ah. 'The appropriate title of Agnostic.'

Charles   Well, it's just C of E for atheist, innit?

Pause.

My grandad was a God-fearing man but my mother said she let go the hand of the Lord during the war. Because of the rationing and the evacuations. She didn't see a banana until she was eleven.

Slight pause.

Said it was 'taking the piss'.

Slight pause.

Sorry.

Vicar   'I gave my heart to know wisdom and to know madness and folly: I perceived that this also is vexation of spirit. For in much wisdom is much grief: and he that increaseth knowledge increaseth sorrow.'

Charles   What does that mean?

Vicar   You are of a generation which searched for self knowledge and identity through science. And it's no surprise when something happens, a fundamental sorrow alights, you find it perplexing.

Charles   So what do I do?

Vicar   Everybody deals with the passing on of a loved one differently.

Charles   On average, what do they do? Any little titbits will do.

Vicar   I can't advise you.

Charles   No, but you could –

Vicar   I listen. Such is the dilemma of faith that there is no advice, only the words of the scriptures. I am not an 'intermediary'. If you wish to petition the Lord, with supplication, you do so directly. You pray.

Charles   So you just –

Vicar   I listen.

Charles   You –

Vicar   I listen and perhaps guide you in –

Charles   Well, why don't you then?

Pause.

Vicar   Perhaps you'd like to come to a congregation. Share your grief.

Charles   Share my grief?

Vicar   Yes.

Charles   Share it with who?

Vicar   The community. Have you not heard 'how good and how pleasant it is for brethren to dwell together in unity'?

Charles   I keep myself to myself.

Vicar   Only the brethren we deserve are manifest.

Charles   How d'you mean?

Vicar   I mean, the people we come to love in this life are only the people we deserve to love.

Charles   'The brethren we deserve are manifest'?

Vicar   Thieves, for example, are thick as thieves because the only people they know are thieves.

Slight pause.

Charles   I like that. Well put, Father . . .

Vicar   Reverend . . .

Charles   Eh?

Vicar   You just converted me. Or promoted me.

Charles   How d'you mean?

Vicar   In an Anglican parish you don't have priests. I'm a vicar.

Charles   Oh.

Pause.

It's quite complicated, innit.

Pause.

D'you think she might be up there watching me?

Vicar   Of course.

Charles   D'you think she's smiling?

Vicar   Yes.

Charles   I bet everybody smiles in the kingdom of Heaven, don't you think, Reverend?

Vicar   Perhaps you'd like something to read.

He hands **Charles** *his Bible.*

Charles   I'll have a bash. Thanks.

The **Vicar** *goes,* **Charles** *examines the Bible.*

Scene Four

Doctor's.

Charles *sits opposite a* **GP** *who makes notes when appropriate.*

Charles   . . . Bus drivers . . . I find myself losing my temper with perfectly normal bus drivers and it's not just because of what happened.

Pause.

Always stopping too late or stopping too early, slamming the brakes on, they drive like they got a club-foot some of them. It just makes me want to hit somebody.

GP   I do understand, Mr Strong.

Charles   They're so careless.

GP   But we all have these trials to contend with. We'd all love to lash out and get things off our chest but we live in a society governed by rules and it's these rules which are holding it together.

Charles   It's doing my head in.

GP   Personally, there's people I'd love to hit. Then I think to myself, 'I'm a doctor . . . My God!' You see?

Pause.

Has anything else been troubling you?

Charles   I'm having nightmares. I dream of finding my mother and father lying murdered in a pool of blood, or I get shot, or the till gets robbed, my car gets stolen . . . I mean, what next?

GP   It's all part of the grieving process. Your mind is probably very restless at the moment.

Charles   You think they're telling me something?

GP   I'm not a psychiatrist.

Charles   Have a stab.

GP   It's more than my job's worth to attempt the work of a specialist.

Pause.

Charles   I've had other dreams. I dream about sex all the time.

GP   Yes.

Charles   Sex with some imaginary woman who I've never met before.

GP   That's perfectly normal.

Charles   I fall in love with her.

GP   Absolutely.

Charles   And she loves me . . .

GP   Of course . . .

Charles   Then I lose her.

GP   Everybody has those dreams. Man has dreamt of the elusive perfect partner since time began. It's a very healthy sign for someone in your position. If you were suffering from depression you might not dream at all.

Pause.

Charles   Then this woman turns into a cat.

GP   I see . . .

Charles   Next thing I know I'm rogering the cat. And it's only afterwards that I realise that this is no ordinary cat but . . . it's my cat.
From when I was a little boy. A tom-cat.

Pause.

I felt so guilty.

Silence.

GP   Obviously you're still quite depressed.
And this gives rise to morbid thoughts.
Questions about the past and guilt about trivial things . . .

Charles   Trivial things . . . how trivial?

GP   It could be anything, things which ordinarily wouldn't trouble you at all.

Pause.

Were you happily married?

Charles   We had the occasional ruck. Who doesn't?

GP   Nothing serious?

Charles   She'd always wanted children.

GP   Did you?

Slight pause.

Charles   Even if we could have had a family . . .

GP   'Even if . . . '?

Pause.

Charles   See, I bought the bar when everybody was buying a place. A year later they're all going into middle management – but I stay put. Her body clock is ticking away and she wants kids and pets and a front lawn and a mortgage and holidays in Orlando . . . and I think that she thought I didn't care about that. But I did care. I cared about her with every drop of life in my body. I cared about her and I adored her more than life itself.

Pause.

But I had a business to run.

Pause.

I told her, 'It beats working for some bastard in a Merc.'

Pause.

That's when I started drinking. On the sauce every other night.

GP   I see.

Charles   Piss-arsed legless every night. Stinking. Senseless.

GP   Mm.

Charles   Shitless. Bombed. Maudlin.

GP   Yes.

Charles   Then I stopped. Just in time.

Pause.

GP   You stopped. Altogether?

Charles   She stopped me.

GP   So you no longer drink.

Charles   I have a glass of wine every now and then.

GP   Shall we say a glass a night?

Charles   More or less.

GP   So, that's seven glasses a week.

*The **GP** scribbles calculations.*

Charles   I have the odd bottle, every now and then.

GP   Maybe a beer after work?

Charles   Couple of beers, yeah.

GP   Spirits?

Charles   Bottle a week maybe.

GP   A week?

Charles *adds up on his fingers. He switches hands and adds up more.*

Charles   Sometimes.

GP   That's more than thirty units a week.

Charles   Yeah, scrub the beer.

GP   Mm, twenty's really the limit.

Charles   I'm good at it. I have a 'strong' constitution.

Laughs. Pause.

GP   Perhaps you need a holiday.

Charles   I don't have time for a holiday.

GP   Have an away day. How often do you exercise?

Charles   Never.

GP   You should try to exercise. It really does help to take your mind off things.

Charles   Does it?

GP   You'd be surprised.

Charles   I am surprised.

GP   Or I could arrange some counselling.

Charles   What about drugs?

GP   Drugs?

Slight pause.

Charles   Pills. I mean proper drugs, I mean, I've heard good reports about, you know, drugs.

GP   I'd give you counselling before I gave you medication.

Charles   Which is better?

GP   That's really up to you to decide.

Charles   Which is quicker?

GP   Ah, the blind faith of man in modern medicine.

Charles   Well, what else is there?

GP Other than counselling?

Charles Yeah.

GP That's up to you as well.

Silence.

Charles This is fucking nonsense.

GP Sorry?

Charles This is rubbish. You're paid to help me.
'Have an away day.'
You're a doctor.

He goes.

Scene Five

Club.

Charles *and the* **Maître d'** *sprawl at a table, drinking coffee and smoking cigarettes.*

Charles Blah blah blah. Blah blah blah. Blah blah blah blah blah.

Pause.

Eh? Innit?

Pause.

Eh? All talk. (*Snorts.*) They're all cunts. 'Have an away day'? (*Snorts.*)

Maître d' Where?

Charles Absolutely. 'Where would you recommend, doc?'

Maître d' No, I'm asking you. Where would you go?

Charles Well, I wouldn't, would I?

Maître d' Why not? Take the doctor's advice.

Pause.

Charles   My dream is to have an away day. What I would give to have an away day. I'd go tomorrow if I had someone to go with.

Maître d'   Go by yourself.

Charles   And someone to hold the fort.

Maître d'   Close for the day.

Charles   No. It wouldn't be the same.

Pause.

A waitress, **Lucy,** *comes over wearing a short skirt, black stockings, suspenders, white blouse and heels. She is carrying a bottle of wine. She shows the* **Maître d'** *the label, he nods, she pours, he tastes, she pours a full glass and he places his hand on her arse.*

Lucy   Oi. I won't tell you again.

Maître d'   What are you going to do?

She exits.

Maître d'   Bugger off to Malaga for the week.

Charles   Turn it in. Malaga?

Maître d'   What's wrong with Malaga?

Charles   Oh, stop. The Costa?

Maître d'   Malaga's not the Costa.

Charles   It's near the Costa.

Maître d'   Well, where do you want to go?

Charles   Somewhere hot.

Maître d'   Florida.

Charles   Camber Sands.

Maître d'   Don't be a cunt. Nobody goes to Camber Sands.

Charles   I used to go to Camber Sands with the missus. She loved it.

Maître d'   Oh, used to . . . certainly. Everybody used to.

Pause.

Charles   You know I can still smell the salt, the odour of salt and sun cream on her skin. Sometimes I smell her perfume. Straight up. I can walk past a bird, a complete stranger, and suddenly bosh. I'm gone. What is that?

Maître d'   Memories.

Charles   Yeah.

Maître d'   I'm so sorry, Charles. If I knew what to say, I'd say it.

Lucy *returns with a bowl of water and puts it on the table. The* **Maître d'** *runs a hand up her leg and she steps back quickly.*

Lucy   Cheeky bugger.

Maître d'   No.

Lucy   That is rude.

Maître d'   Is it?

Lucy   Yeah.

Maître d'   What are you going to do about it?

Lucy   God.

She exits. **Charles** *sniffs the air.*

Charles   Eh?

Maître d'   Oh, stop.

Charles   Eh?

Maître d'   Turn it in.

Charles   Why? I'm single.

Maître d'   Charles, come on. It's undignified.

Lucy *returns wearing a black gown and mortar-board like a public school teacher and carrying a pepper-mill. She puts her foot on the chair and grinds pepper into the bowl. He puts a hand on her knee. He runs his hand up her leg to her crotch. She slaps him and takes her foot off the chair abruptly.*

Maître d' Ow.

Lucy That's naughty.

Maître d' What did you do that for?

Lucy I should send you to detention.

Maître d' That hurt.

Lucy I should –

Maître d' Use the cane, the cane.

Lucy Oh yeah. Whoops.

She extracts a cane from her waistline. **Maître d'** *stands and bends over.* **Lucy** *hesitates, then smacks his arse.*

Maître d' Harder.

She smacks harder.

Lucy Like that?

Maître d' Spaghetti.

Lucy 'Please may I have . . .'

Maître d' 'Please may I have my main course now.'

Lucy Certainly, sir.

She exits. He rubs his cheek, sighs, sits. Pause.

Charles How long you been in this lark then?

Maître d' It's the new thing, Charlie.

Charles Really?

Pause.

How long have we known each other?

Maître d' Years.

Charles Well, I'm glad you're around. Because I'm telling you, we live in a world of jobsworths. A world of people with no guts. No soul. But I can come here, any time of the day or night and you always listen.

Lucy *returns with a plate heaped with elastic bands.*

Maître d'   What's this?

Lucy   Your spaghetti.

Maître d'   Elastic bands. I said spaghetti.

Lucy   Spaghetti is elastic bands.

Maître d'   Spaghetti is shoe-laces. Elastic bands is green salad. What's dessert?

Lucy   Summer pudding.

Maître d'   No, what represents dessert? What's summer pudding?

Lucy   Sponges?

Maître d'   Sponge scourers.

Lucy   You want me to fetch dessert?

Maître d'   No just . . . put that down.

She puts down the plate.

What are you wearing underneath your gown?

Slight pause.

Lucy   Wouldn't you like to know?

Maître d'   I do know, for Christ's sake. You're wearing your fucking blouse, aren't you? Remove your blouse when you don the gown in future.
Do you want to learn this or not?

Lucy   Yeah.

Maître d'   How many times have we been through this?
You've been at it a week and you can't carry out the simplest instructions.

She doesn't respond.

Do you know how many girls would give their eye teeth to work here?

She starts to go.

Take my plate.

As she takes it he grabs her around the waist and puts a hand down her cleavage.

Maître d' (*growls*).

She struggles, he holds tight, she slaps him and breaks away.

Ow! Stop doing that!

Lucy   You're supposed to like it.

Maître d'   Use the cane for fuck's sake!

Lucy   It was only a slap.

He stands clutching his cheek.

Maître d'   Never hit people in the head! OK? You'll knock somebody out.

He sits. She leans over to get the plate, he pinches her bottom, she steps back and pulls out the cane.

Maître d'   OK, fine. Now what do you say?

Lucy   'Would you like to go to detention?'

Maître d'   OK. 'No, thank you.'

He holds out a fifty-pound note. She doesn't take it.

Lucy   What's this?

Maître d' (*sighs*)   It's your 'tip'.

She reaches out to take it and he drops it on the floor, sweeps it under the table with his foot.

Well, do you want it or not?

Lucy   No, thank you very much.

Maître d'   You don't need an extra nifty?

Charles   My God, is that the time?

Lucy   No.

Maître d'   On your wages? Must be joking.

Charles   I best be off, eh?

Maître d'   No, you're all right.

Lucy   I think I'd prefer it behind the bar.

Maître d'   Pick it up.

Charles   Places to go, people to see.

Maître d'   Get under the table and pick it up, you bitch!

Charles   Uh, listen, old son . . .

Maître d' (*to* **Charles**)   In a minute.

Lucy *gets under the table on hands and knees.* **Charles** *stands and paces, embarrassed. The* **Maître d'** *rolls his eyes, and gestures with his hand.*

And so on and so forth. That's fine. Any questions?

Lucy   I've had enough of this.

She starts to go.

Maître d'   Now what?

Lucy   I'm not that type of woman.

He laughs slightly.

Maître d'   What type are you?
Come on.

Pause.

Lucy   I'm shy.

Maître d'   'Shy'? Men like shy women.

Lucy   I don't know what I'm doing.

Maître d'   Men like women who don't know what they're doing.

Lucy   It's driving me mad.

Maître d'   Men like mad women.

Charles   Mad women are great . . .

Maître d'   The point is, you're not really mad. You're not really shy.

Lucy I'm not a prostitute.

Maître d' Hey Hey Hey!

Pause. They all look at each other. **Charles** *goes and waits by the door.*

I can't afford to keep losing people. It makes the clientele jumpy.

Lucy The clientele are already jumpy.

Maître d' You belong here. Take a day off and you'll come back refreshed.

Lucy (*tuts*).

She goes.

Maître d' Lucy, you come back here.

She reaches the door.

If you walk out that door you'll regret it.

She exits.

If you're not back in twenty-four hours you'll regret it.

Charles *fidgets. Snorts. 'Growls.'*

Silence.

Charles *starts to go.*

Maître d' Nice to see you again, Charles. Stay in touch.

Charles We'll have a bevvie.

Maître d' When I'm not so busy, perhaps.

Charles *exits.*

Scene Six

Bar.

Charles *stands behind the bar.* **Lucy** *sits on a stool on the other side of the bar.*

Lucy . . . So when the clientele misbehaved you had to smack 'em. Thing was, the more you smacked 'em the more they misbehaved, the dirty old sods.

Charles (*snorts*) Ridiculous.

Lucy Nah, that was the fun bit.

Charles How d'you mean?

Lucy Makes a change to be dishing it out for once. (*Laughs.*)

Charles How d'you mean?

Lucy Nothing.

Pause.

I wasn't very good at it.

Pause.

D'you have music?

Charles No.

Lucy Why not?

Charles It's a boozer. People come here to booze.

Lucy Oh.

Pause.

Charles What was he paying you?

Lucy Tenner an hour plus tips.

Charles More than you'll get here.

Lucy It's the principle, isn't it?

Charles Where d'you live?

Lucy Tooting Bec. Next door to the Lido.

Charles Classy.

Lucy Nah, it's just a bedsit.

Charles It's quite a walk away.

Lucy I don't mind.

Slight pause.

Charles   You're not a student, are you?

Lucy   Do I look like a student?

Charles   I can't have you pissing off to become a geologist all of a sudden.

Lucy   Nah, been in catering since school, haven't I?

Charles   Get your thingies, did you?

Lucy   How d'you mean?

Charles   Qualifications. A levels.

Lucy   All that. Yeah.

Charles   You've got A levels?

Lucy   Absolutely . . . lots.

Charles   And you wanna work in a pub?

Pause.

Lucy   Actually . . . I packed it in when I was fifteen.

Charles   How come?

Lucy   I was expelled.

Charles   What for?

Lucy   Oh . . . I don't know . . . something trivial.
(*Laughs.*) Stealing. Arson.

Charles   Oh, stop.

Lucy   Alcoholism. Drugs.

Charles   I'll get the giggles.

They laugh.

Pause.

Lucy   No, I was just being difficult, I expect. You know,
'immature'.

Charles   As long as you can pull a pint.

Lucy   Absolutely.

Charles   When can you start?

Lucy   When d'you want me to start?

Charles   Tomorrow.

Lucy   I can start today.

Charles   Tomorrow's better. I've got a bit of business to sort out. I'll show you out.

Lucy   What sort of business?

Charles   It's personal. Don't worry, I'm not going under.

He comes around from behind the bar.

My wife just died. I'm tending the grave today.

Lucy   Oh. I'm sorry.

Charles   No, you're all right.

Lucy   Just making sure.

Charles   It's six quid an hour. You keep your tips, you don't have to spank nobody, no dope fiends, coke-heads, suits or lunatics. D'you want the job or not?

Lucy   'Course.

She joins him at the door.

Charlie   Tomorrow then?

Lucy   Yeah. See you.

She goes.

Charles   Hey.

She comes back.

D'you like rum?

He picks up a bottle from a crate by the door.

Lucy   Not really.

Charles   It's booze, isn't it?

Lucy   I don't drink.

Charles   Why not?

Lucy   I just don't.

Charles   Very wise.

She goes. **Charles** *puts the bottle back.*

Scene Seven

Cemetery.

Charles *places flowers on his wife's grave and stares at it. Nearby a* **Woman** *places flowers on another grave. She sees* **Charles**.

Woman   Hullo. I didn't see you there.

Charles   Hullo. All right?

Woman   Don't I know you?

Charles   Boozer in Garratt Lane.

Woman   I thought you looked familiar.
Who brings you here, if you don't mind me asking?

Charles   My wife. The funeral was on the weekend.

Woman   Oh, shame. Hot or cold?

Charles   How d'you mean?

Woman   Cremated or embalmed?

Charles   Embalmed.

Pause.

Woman   I read where they were supposed to cremate Albert Einstein. Then somebody came along and pinched his brain. Sliced the top of his head clean off like a lid and whipped it out. It's in three pieces now, pickled, somewhere in America.

Charles   Really?

Woman   Yes.

Pause. **Charles** *stares at his wife's grave.*

They took his eyes as well. Yes. Sucked them out with a . . . a sucker and kept them in a jam jar. Like the pope's relics, you know. It's bonkers.

Charles *looks at the* **Woman**.

Charles   Bonkers, yeah.

Woman   I'm up the pub after this. Fancy a stiff drink. You're welcome to join me.

Pause.

If you needed some company, that's all I meant.

Pause.

Because you're a very attractive man.

Pause.

It's probably a bit early, I suppose.

Charles   How'd you mean?

Woman   They say it takes three months before you finish mourning properly.

Charles   Three months?

Woman   Well, it all depends on your character, really.

Charles   Character, yeah.

Woman   Your nature.

Charles   Yeah.

Woman   And sometimes it's just not . . . not in your nature. Mind you, if you can bring yourself to be positive about it, the world's your oyster.

Charles   Absolutely.

Pause.

What if you can't?

Woman   Oh, I don't know.

Charles   Dear-oh-dear.

They laugh slightly.

Woman   'Dear-oh-dear', precisely.

She goes.

Scene Eight

Bar.

Closing time. **Charles** *is standing behind the bar, holding a baseball bat and examining it.* **Lucy** *walks in carrying a stack of glasses and whistling. She puts the glasses on the bar.*

Charles   Everybody gone?

Lucy   Yeah.

Charles   That was quick.

Lucy   I've got the touch.

Charles   Cop hold of this.

He hands her the baseball bat.

Lucy   What's this for?

Charles   Guess.

Lucy   I hate to think.

Charles   From time to time people misbehave.

Lucy   I'm not doing any funny stuff.

Charles   You don't have to use it, just look like you know how to.

He brandishes it threateningly.

Lucy   What if it doesn't work?

Charles   Then you have to use it.

Lucy   I wouldn't know where to start.

Charles   I'll show you.

Lucy   Why can't you get a bouncer or something?

Charles   I am the bouncer, love.
And when I'm not here, you're the bouncer.

Lucy   You're making me nervous.

Charles   There's a lot of funny people out there.

He has a few practice swings.

Lucy   You're bloody joking. Anything could happen.

Charles   Like what?

Lucy   I could miss.

Charles   Not if you learn properly. Now, you keep it under
the bar resting in this crate so you can grab it quick. The minute
anybody starts anything you grab it like so . . . and so . . . rest it
on the bar and 'bang'. You slide it across the bar into his guts.
Watch.

He demonstrates the manoeuvre.

Lift . . . and slide. And you want to get him in the solar plexus,
just below the rib cage because you want to wind him, double
him up. Then you come round and you get him on the ground.

He comes around from behind the bar.

Work on his body with clean, crisp smacks. Concentrate on the
pressure points. Backs of the knees, elbows, ankles. Because you
want to immobilise him. Yeah?

Lucy   Yeah . . .

Charles   Surprise him. You have a go.

She goes behind the bar and tries the manoeuvre.

Lucy   Lift . . . and slide. Lift and . . . slide.

Charles   Faster. See, it's all in the wrist. In your technique.

Lucy *practises,* **Charles** *watches.*

Charles   'Cause you want to break his ribs. Get to his vital organs. Teach the fucker a lesson! Go on . . . !

Charles *suddenly stares into space.* **Lucy** *stops.*

Lucy   Are you all right?

Charles   What am I saying?

Pause.

What am I like? Eh?

Pause. They look at each other.

Lucy   You look tired.

Charles   It's been a long day.

Pause.

Lucy   You miss her, don't you?

Charles   She was the sweetest, loveliest little girl I ever knew.

Pause.

Not a nasty bone in her body.

Pause.

You know the one thing she loved more than anything else in the world?

Lucy   What's that?

Charles   Her garden.
Clumping about the garden with her little boots on, her hair all over the gaff, growing things. She was magic with courgettes. She had a gift for courgettes. And her flowers. Not ordinary flowers. Special flowers. Rare, odd, funny coloured things. She had style. Yellow crocus. Clematis. Blue irises. Purple irises.

Pause. He puts the bat away.

You hungry?

Lucy   Starved.

Charles   Fancy a Chinese?

Scene Nine

Chinese restaurant.

Charles *and* **Lucy** *raise their glasses, smile and so on.* **Charles** *watches* **Lucy** *eat.*

Charles   You remind me of her.

Lucy   Who?

Charles   My wife.

Lucy   I've heard that before.

She stops eating.

Sorry.

Charles   When she was young.

Lucy   Ah.

They eat.

I want to get married one day. I think it must be nice to, you know, always, you know, have somebody there.

Charles   Absolutely.

Lucy   Somebody to keep you warm at night and all that.

Charles   Yes.

Lucy   Somebody to listen to all your silly ideas. Tell you you done the right thing when you done the wrong thing. That's romance, that is. That's what love is.

Pause.

Charles   You don't have a fella then?

Lucy   He's a fucking animal. I mean it. If he walked through that door right now I'd murder him.

Charles   Ah.

Lucy   Sadistic bastard. I hate him.

Pause.

Actually he's your mate from the club. It was just a fling, really. You must think I'm such a slapper.

Pause.

I know he does.

Charles   I don't.

Lucy   He does.

Charles   I'm sure he doesn't.

Lucy   He does.

Charles *stops eating and pats* **Lucy**'*s hand across the table. They look at each other. He takes his hand away.*

Charles   Sorry.

Lucy   I'm not, you know.

Charles   I didn't say you were.

Lucy   Your fucking wife just died.

Charles   I was only ...

Lucy   What are you like, eh? Mad?

She prods **Charles**'*s food with chopsticks, lifts a mouthful to her mouth and eats.*

Call this chicken chow mein? Chicken shavings more like. I bet you they've got one chicken chained up out the back and they just shave bits off of it and mix 'em in with a noodle or two, fucking skinflints. Aren't you hungry?

Charles   No.

Lucy   Oh.

She stops eating. Wipes her mouth with a napkin.

Pause.

Charles   I'll get the bill.

Lucy   Bill, bill good idea.

Charles (*to* **Waiter**)   Waiter ...

Lucy (*to* **Waiter**)   Yoo-hoo, waiter ...

Silence.

Charles   So. You all right to open up tomorrow?

Lucy   Absolutely.

Charles   Smashing.

Scene Ten

Bar.

The **Maître d'** *lies on the floor in a pool of blood.* **Lucy** *is still clutching the baseball bat in horror.* **Charles** *is squatting down feeling for a pulse.*

Charles   Jesus.

Lucy   Where were you?

Charles   I had things to do.

Lucy   I was waiting for you all day.

Charles   What did you let him in for?

Lucy   He wouldn't go away. He was hammering the door down.

Charles   Fuck.

Charles *goes and locks the door.*

Lucy   Then he started going on about how much he missed me and how sorry he was and how nice I was and how sensible I was. Then he got frisky.

Charles   Frisky?

Lucy   He started threatening me.

Charles   So you let him in?

Lucy   Yeah.

Charles   After he started threatening you?

Lucy   Yeah ...

Pause.

Charles   You got a mirror?

Lucy   I've got a compact.

Charles   That'll do.

She exits and returns with a handbag from which she extracts the compact. She gives it to **Charles** *who blows on it and rubs it on his shirt.*

Charles   Covered in shit.

He breathes on it. Taps it.

Covered in powder.

He holds it to the **Maître d'**s *mouth.*

Hang about.

He polishes it. Tries again. He hands it back to **Lucy** *and stands.*

Long pause.

Lucy   I was scared.

Charles   I'm scared now. What were you thinking?

Lucy   He had a knife. I panicked.

Charles   What sort of knife?

Lucy   A little one. With a . . . a pearl handle.

Charles   So he attacked you with a knife?

Lucy   He was about to.

Charles   Did he or didn't he?

Lucy   He really lost his temper. He had that look about him. He had that look in his eyes. He was about to snap . . .

Charles (*pause*)   Has he . . . has he done anything like this before?

Lucy   No. It was a complete surprise.

Charles *fetches a cloth and wipes up the blood.*

Lucy   You don't believe me, do you? You think I'm just being neurotic. Well, don't you?

Pause.

It was an accident. I didn't mean to hurt him.

Charles   You hit him in the head.

Lucy   I was trying to stun him.

Charles (*scrubbing*)   What did I tell you about that, Lucy? You weren't listening, were you? I told you precisely what to do, if there's a problem, we went through the whole procedure, but no, you had a better idea.

He goes behind the bar, wipes his hands and finds a bottle of rum. Opens it and drinks.

I leave you alone for five minutes . . .

Lucy   Oh, don't go on about it!

Charles *goes to the phone on the wall and dials.*

Lucy   What are you doing?

Charles   Phoning the police.

She goes to him and they briefly struggle over the phone.

Lucy   They won't believe me.

Charles   This isn't a game.

Lucy   . . . And it was your idea anyway. You told me to do it. I wouldn't do a thing like that in a million years.

Pause. He puts the phone down.

We could say you did it. Because you were depressed.

Pause.

Charles   Why?

Pause.

People will miss him. His family. His friends.

Lucy   He doesn't have any friends. We're his friends.

Charles   People will come looking for him. People . . . in the community.

Lucy   Who?

Silence.

Charles   Well, what are we going to do with him?

Lucy   We could throw him in the river.

Charles   No.

He picks up the phone and dials.

Lucy   We could bury him on Balham Common. It's a bit more appropriate.

Pause.

And, and easier . . .

Charles   Oh, shut up. Just shut up.

Lucy   It's all winos and hookers. Nobody'll find him.

Charles   We're not doing it.

Lucy   Why not?

Charles   Because it's wrong!

Pause.

And we could get caught.

And then I'll go to prison because it's my bar and my baseball bat and I'm the oldest.

Pause.

How far is Balham Common?

Lucy   Ten minutes in the car.

Pause.

Have you got a car?

He just looks at her, still holding the phone.

Scene Eleven

Balham Common.

Evening. **Charles** *and* **Lucy** *lower the corpse, wrapped in a blanket, into the grave.*

Lucy   He was a vicious, pitiless bastard. He deserved it.

Charles   Much as I liked him, he was a pimp.

Lucy   Yeah.

Charles   I'm glad he's dead.

Lucy   Me too.

Charles   If a man can't play by the rules then he deserves every dark fucking day that befalls him.

Pause.

He wants to come into my place, with a knife, start throwing his weight around, he's got no manners, then it's not my problem.

Pause.

The good Lord giveth and He taketh and we, God bless us, made in His image, do the same and so fuck it.

Pause.

It makes me so angry, Lucy.

Lucy   D'you think we should say a prayer or something?

Charles   What sort of prayer?

Lucy   I don't know.

He looks at her, then pulls his Bible out of his coat pocket and flips through it. After a moment, he shuts it and hands it to **Lucy**.

Charles   Go on.

Lucy *looks through the Bible, shuts it and hands it back.* **Charles** *puts it in his pocket, takes out a flask of rum and drinks. He puts the flask away and fills in the grave.* **Lucy** *gazes at the corpse.*

Lucy   He doesn't look dead.

Pause.

Lucy   What if he isn't? I mean, you're not a doctor.

Charles *stops work.*

Lucy   What if I tell someone? You know what I'm like.

Charles *gets back to work. Pause.*

Lucy   I've seen a few dead bodies in my time.

Charles   Really.

Lucy   My aunty died when I was thirteen. I saw her in her casket. She was yellow. And sort of waxy. Her skin looked like wax.

Charles   Sometimes they use wax if there's any wounds.

Lucy   There wasn't any wounds.

Charles   They drain the blood out which is what makes the skin go yellow.

Lucy   She gassed herself. Stuck her head in the oven. It was sad. She was always so cheerful and positive about things.

Pause.

I've known a lot of people who've died suddenly.

Charles   I haven't.

Lucy   Well, you're older. It's different for you.

Charles   Is it?

Lucy   Different generation. People do more now, don't they? Experience more.
Take more risks. Then there's suicides.
Everybody I know knows somebody who's either thought about it or tried it or actually done it.

Charles   Yes, all right.

Lucy   Live life while you can, when you can, as fast you can. Within reason. That's my motto.

He stops work.

Charles   What is the matter with you?

Lucy   D'you think there is something the matter with me?

Charles   Yes.

Lucy   What?

Charles   I don't know.

Charles *works*.

Lucy   Nearly finished?

Charles *flings the shovel down*.

Charlie   Are you thick or something?

Lucy   No.

Charles   Well, what is it?

Lucy   I don't know.

Charles *tramps down the dirt*.

Lucy   I expect this means I'm out of a job.

Pause.

I didn't have to stay you know, I could have fucked off home hours ago.

Charles   Why didn't you?

Lucy   I don't know. I'd be bored.

Charles   We should open up. It'll look suspicious.

Pause.

Get in the car.

Lucy   Are you sure?

Charles   Get in the car before I change my mind. In the . . . in the front.

Lucy   How d'you mean?

Charles   In the front where I can keep my eye on you.

Lucy   I'm not a child.

Charles   I know that.

Pause.

Lucy   Why are you doing this?

Charles   Stop asking questions.

Lucy   I want to know why.

Charles   Because I want to.

Lucy   Just tell me why.

Charles *picks up the blanket and folds it carefully.*

Charles   I don't know why.

She goes. He looks at the grave, picks up the shovel and goes.
Blackout.

Act Two

Scene One

Charles's *flat.*

Charles *is sitting on a bed, holding a phone and drinking from a tumbler. A bottle sits nearby.*

Charles   Mum?

Slight pause.

Dad, it's me. Charles.

Pause.

I'm all right. Yeah.

Pause.

It was all right. It was nice.

Pause.

Dozens. Yes. She was a popular girl.
Yes, she was lovely. I know that.

Pause.

Very pretty.

Pause.

It was a lovely day, yes.

Pause.

Lovely. Nice and hot.

Slight pause.

Smashing. All week. Beautiful. Listen, Dad . . . No, don't get mum just yet. I want to talk to you.

Pause.

I just want to talk. See how you are.

Pause.

Who? Which side?

Pause.

He packs a chiv, I know. He's a cunt.

Slight pause.

His son's a cunt as well.

Slight pause.

They're a pair of cunts. The uncle's a cunt with glasses. Which makes him a glunt, yeah, very funny, Dad . . . I know they drink here but I never make them welcome. No, he's in Parkhurst – oh, really . . . ? Look, apart from that – you're well in yourself, yeah? Cutting down on the fags?

Pause.

And mum? No, don't go and get her. I want to talk to you. I just want to . . . all right put her on.

Pause.

Hullo, Mum. How are you?

Long pause.

I know he is, Mum . . . Friday . . . got a keg of spillage especially for him. Parkhurst.

Pause.

The funeral was lovely. Lovely day, yes . . . how are you, you, Mum? Never mind me.

Pause.

Marvellous. That's all I wanted to hear. I have to go now.

Slight pause.

Nothing's wrong. I'm just tired.

Slight pause.

You're absolutely right, Mum. Housework?
No. Can't say that I have been.

Pause.

I don't want a new girlfriend. You're absolutely ... but ... oh, good plan, Mum.

Pause.

No, I'm just a bit ... 'sad', yeah.

Pause.

No ... no ... no ... something happened in the bar and what with one thing and another ...

Slight pause.

Three square meals a day, Mum. You're absolutely right. Yes, Mum. I have to go now, Mum. Y – all right. Ta ta. Ta ta. Love to dad. Ta ta.

He hangs up and drinks.

Scene Two

Bar.

A lock-in is in progress. Music plays. **Lucy** *and fellow* **Drinkers** *sing along drunkenly.* **Charles** *wipes the bar and clears up.*

Drinkers   When no one else can understand me
                When everything I do is wrong
                You give me hope and consolation
                You give me strength to carry on

Lucy *(simultaneously)*   Join in, Charlie.

He doesn't.

Drinkers   And you're always there to lend a hand
                In everything I do
                That's the wonder, the wonder of you
                Da de da, da de da, da de da ...

Charles *turns the music off. He opens a bottle of rum and drinks from the bottle.*

Silence.

Woman   Charlie Charlie Charlie Charlie Charlie . . . This man . . . is a . . . where did my glass go?

Drinker One   Hello, cheeky chops . . .

Lucy   I don't remember your name.

Drinker Two   I planted my wife a week after my fortieth birthday. I stood around the grave with the in-laws discussing the weather . . .

Drinker One   Forgotten already?

Woman   Leave her alone, she's only little.

Drinker Two   Her mother had a smile like a thin streak of piss . . .

Drinker One   I think you are a dangerous woman.

Drinker Two   The old man had regressed into a sort of childlike hysteria somewhere around the third day of his honeymoon and hadn't spoken since . . .

Woman   Ignore him, pet, he's been in Parkhurst the past five years . . .

Lucy   No! What did you do?

Silence.

Sorry.

Pause.

I wasn't being funny.

Drinker One *laughs suddenly*.

Drinker One   What a character!

Lucy   I wasn't saying anything or anything . . .

Drinker One   Isn't she a character, Charles?

Woman   You leave her alone, you big hairy bastard, she don't know.

Drinker Two   The heavens pissed buckets and I stared into the hole and reflected on the banality that had gone before . . .

Lucy   I was just interested.

Drinker One   Never ask me that again.

Lucy   I won't.

Drinker Two   . . . . And the banality that was to come.

Drinker One   Have I met you before? You remind me of someone.

Pause.

Lucy   I've heard that before.

Woman   Don't take any notice of him, love, he's a pervert.

Drinker One   Listen to me, no listen – you are a devastatingly handsome young woman. Devastatingly . . .

Lucy   Oh, stop . . .

Woman   Should pick on somebody his own age . . .

Lucy   'A devastatingly handsome young . . . '?

Woman   Live your life, girl, that's what you should do.

Lucy   He's asking for it, isn't he? Eh?

Charles   Lucy . . .

Lucy   Come on, then. Let's have you.

Charles   Please . . .

Drinker Two   'I'm a Captain of fucking Industry,' I thought. 'But I still shit in a toilet and like everybody else I'm going to die.'

Drinker One   I'm not being funny, I'm attracted to you.

Drinker Two   And the funeral bells tolled and a Mockingbird sang as if to . . .

Lucy   I'll bury you.

Drinker One (*laughing*)   Priceless!

Woman   Don't say that, girl, it's bad luck!

Lucy   I killed somebody, I did.

Woman   Don't say that, girl, someone might believe you!

Lucy   Charles dug a hole and buried the body for me.

Drinker One (*laughing*)   Oh, my sainted aunty.

Drinker Two   'I looked, and behold a pale horse and his name that sat on him was Death, and Hell followed with him . . .'

Woman   No, you are joking!

Lucy   Yes – no!

Drinker Two   Which is to say, 'The shit is really going to hit the fan now.'

Lucy   He died right there, right where you're all standing.

Drinker One   Is this true, Charlie? Little girl says you and her stiffed a geezer.

Silence.

Woman   Not the wife, you mean?

Lucy   No, somebody else.

Drinker One   Oh, stop! I'll have a bloody heart attack in a minute.

Pause.

Woman   You're pulling our legs.

Lucy   It's true.

Drinker Two   This is unbelievable.

Woman   How did you kill him?

Drinker One   This is my type of lady.

Lucy   I hit him.

Drinker One   Chinned him? That's the stuff.

Lucy   I beat the shit out of him.

Drinker Two   Outrageous.

Woman   What, a drunk?

Lucy   Actually . . .

Drinker One   'Actually, *actually*.' Go on.

Pause.

Lucy   You won't believe me.

Drinker One   You're all right . . . say it.

Lucy   No.

Drinker One   Say it.

Woman   What, what say what?

Lucy   Don't laugh.

Slight pause.

He was my lover.

Woman   No . . .

Lucy   Yes.

Woman   Fuck off . . .

Lucy   Fucking done him in because . . .

Woman   Is this true, Charlie?

Drinker One   Classic . . .

Lucy   Because he was hurting me . . .

Drinker One (*laughing*)   Absolutely.

Drinker Two   And you got away with it?

Lucy   It's not funny.

Drinker One   This is hysterical!

Lucy   Tell 'em, Charlie. Charles . . .

Charles *stares into space.*

Pause.

Lucy   Are you going to vomit?

Woman   Get a bucket, someone . . .

Lucy   Charles, what's wrong?

Woman   Quick, Charlie's gonna vomit.

The **Woman** *goes behind the bar and comes back with a bucket. She waits with the bucket.*

Lucy   I feel awful.

Charles (*to* **Lucy**)   You're drunk.

Drinker One   Aha! I thought so. I could tell.

Woman   What did he say? What was that?

Charles   Don't fuck about.

Lucy   The poor man.

Charles   Don't say another word.

Woman   Did she or didn't she?

Lucy   I am such a bitch.

Charles   Do you hear me? Do You Understand?

Woman   I won't tell anyone, I promise. Come on, Charlie . . . Charles . . . ?

Pause.

Charles   Believe what you want to believe.

Pause.

Woman   What are you like, eh? Did he try and touch you up?

Drinker Two   I do not believe this. She admits to slaughtering a living person on this exact spot . . .

Drinker One   Watch it . . .

Drinker Two   What was his name?

Woman   Oh, you can't ask that . . .

Drinker Two   No, we have a right to know . . .

Drinker One Oh, do we? How jolly.

Charles SHUT UP!

Pause.

Who are you people? What do you know about anything? You come here every night and drink and piss and moan and laugh and line up like so many pigs at a fucking trough. You're ignorant.

Silence.

Woman You've upset him now.

Charles What's it like to be so fancy-free, eh? Nothing whatsoever occupying your minds. Come on, I'm interested.

A long pause. **Lucy** *goes to* **Charles**.

Woman So. How long have you two known each other?

Charles Get out. Go on. Piss off, the lot of you.

Pause.

Charles *stands and 'fronts'* **Drinker One**. *Pause.*

Drinker One Don't do anything you'll regret, Charlie-boy.

Pause. The **Drinkers** *slowly file out.* **Charles** *sits.* **Lucy** *sits too and holds his hand.*

Lucy Shh. It's all right. I'll look after you.

Scene Three

Seaside.

Lucy *and* **Charles** *sit in deck-chairs side by side on the sea front. The sound of gulls overhead.*

Lucy Cup of tea?

Charles Lovely.

She pours a cup from a flask and hands it to him. Pours her own cup and they sip.

Lucy   Digestive?

Charles   Ta.

She hands him a biscuit.

Lucy   Holiday.

Charles   Lovely. Thank you.

Lucy   It's a pleasure.

Charles   Yeah.

Pause.

My old man says if you've got one friend in this life you're a lucky man. One person who you can still trust, when you're eighty years old, then you're a lucky man.

Pause.

You know, the one person he listens to? And the one person who listens to him? My dear old mum.

Lucy   Bless 'em.

Charles   Bless 'em. 'As long as you have your health,' she'd say, 'as long as you're still alive and still half-sane, what more can you expect? Eh? Keep things simple. Because the human race, son, is not worth a flying fucking bag of nuts.'

Pause.

Lucy   My parents divorced when I was ten. Spent most of the time 'round my aunty's.

Charles   Oh, I'm sorry.

Lucy   I never liked them. Too quiet.

Charles   Yeah.

Lucy   Not very affectionate.

Charles   No.

Lucy   Not much fun at all really.

Pause.

Still, I don't suppose parents are meant to be fun, are they?

Slight pause.

They're meant to be dignified.

Pause.
They link arms.
They look at each other.
They kiss.

Charles Bloody hell.

Lucy Whoops.

Charles Sorry –

Lucy No –

Charles I –

Lucy I –

Charles You . . .

Pause.

Lucy Isn't it a lovely . . . windy day?

Charles Lovely.

Pause.

Lucy You must think I'm such a slapper.

Charles Don't say that.

Lucy I'm not.

Charles Why do you say these things?

Lucy I don't know.

Charles No, why? I really want to know.

Long pause.

Lucy They say people do this after a trauma.

Pause.

You become closer to people. Out of relief. It's like you realise how lucky you are.

Charles   It was . . . it was inevitable.

Scene Four

Hotel.

Charles *is lying in bed.* **Lucy** *comes into the room wearing only knickers and bra. She has a towel around her head. She takes the towel off her head and shakes her wet hair loose. Sits on the end of the bed and brushes her hair. She applies talcum powder to her body.* **Charles** *watches.*

Charles   You know what I'm turning into? An unprincipled man.

Pause.

I find it easier to take a long hard look at myself after a good shag.

Lucy (*tuts*)   You're in a jolly mood all of a sudden.

Charles   I was just thinking how lovely it is to watch a woman dress. I'm not being funny. I used to watch my wife getting dressed in the mornings. Doing her hair, rubbing in the talcum powder. Makes being alive worthwhile.

Pause.

She was extremely clean. Always filling the bathroom with special little soaps and all sorts of new scents and smells. Always grooming herself. I got quite a kick out of watching her shave her legs. Legs, armpits, marvellous.

Lucy *puts on a sweater.*

Lucy   Really?

Charles   Yes.

Lucy *picks up a skirt and goes to the window. She opens the curtains and window and stands looking out, holding the skirt.*

Charles   I remember our honeymoon. I remember her sitting on the bed in the hotel, with the sun and the sea-air streaming in and her skin and her wet hair all golden in the light, gulls cawing in the distance, and I thought to myself, What does this mean? Eh? This is the only thing that matters.
Fuck work. I'm a cunt.

Pause.

We were in love. Love's great. Love wears a white hat.

Lucy   Are you going to get up or are you going to just stare at my arse all morning?

Charles   Come here, babe.

Lucy   Oh, stop. You're not going to get all soppy on me, are you?

Charles   I already have, girl.

Lucy   Because you know that was just a fuck, don't you?

Slight pause.

Charles   How d'you mean?

Lucy   A quick fuck to keep our spirits up.

Charles   It worked.

Lucy   It doesn't mean anything.

Charles   Really?

Lucy   Because you know this is what ruins friendships, isn't it?

Charles   I know.

Lucy   And we don't want that to happen, do we?

Charles   No ... of course.

Lucy   I don't want anybody getting the wrong end of the stick.

Charles   Who?

Lucy   You. I couldn't cope with another fiasco.

Pause.

Charles   Well, they certainly broke the mould when they made you.

Pause.

I nev . . . I never know whether to laugh or cry.

She goes to him.

Lucy   Look at you.
Big fat belly, hairy arse, toe-nails need cutting, you stink, boozer's breath, hungover again, big hairy bollocks like a gorilla, big ugly cock, look at it, look at all those veins. You haven't got a pot to piss in, no future, you're moody, ugly, bad tempered, old . . .

She kisses him.

What do you want for breakfast?

She puts her skirt on.

Charles   Toast?

Lucy *picks up the phone by the bed, dials, and clears her throat.*

Lucy   Toast for room nine.

She hangs up.

Scene Five

Bar.

Lucy *is working behind the bar.* **Drinker One** *is sitting at the bar with a drink, drunk.*

Drinker   Drink?

Pause.

I'm having one. You're not busy.

Lucy   You're drunk.

Drinker   Eh?

Lucy   No more drinks.

Drinker   Eh?

Lucy   You're drunk. No more.

Drinker   What is it? Rum and Coke?

Lucy   I won't tell you again.

Drinker   Just a tipple.

Lucy (*tuts*).

Drinker   You know what I like about this stuff? When you drink, the world's still out there, it just doesn't have you by the balls.

Lucy   Oh, absolutely.

Pause.

Drinker   I always wanted to own a fancy wine emporium. A fancy one in the Fulham Road perhaps, or New Malden. As a matter of fact, I was once mooted for a job with Balls Brothers. Only they said I was an alcoholic. Wound up running the Cash 'n' Carry in Wandsworth. Briefly. Before my incarceration.

Lucy   Really?

Drinker   Mm.

Lucy   I *say*.

She yawns. Pause.

Drinker   You know what I like about you? You're always here. I like that. Makes you feel that there are things that are at least a little constant in this world, you know what I'm saying?

Lucy   I would be, wouldn't I?

Drinker   Of course.

Lucy   I'm the barmaid.

Drinker   True.

Lucy   It's my job.

Drinker *nods and stares into his drink.*

Pause.

Drinker   Sad about the guvnor's wife.

Pause.

Well, he wasn't to know, was he?

Pause.

That's what married life is about. The good times and the bad.
So long as you have your health and you don't hate each other's
guts by the end then you're on top, in my book.

Lucy   What you on about?

Drinker (*tuts*)   The things they used to say about each other.
My goodness. Always squabbling and carrying on like a pair of
kids. Always rucking, like Tom and Jerry they was. I saw them
in Northcote Road market one day, strolling about, hand in
hand, bold as brass, and her with a pair of black eyes like a
fucking racoon.

Pause.

That's what she was like, see. Spirited. Very emotionally strong
and very lively before the separation ...

Lucy   I beg your pardon?

Drinker   I was just saying ...

Lucy   I think you've said enough.

Drinker   Funny bloke, Charles. He's a lovely man. One of the
best. But you know the only trouble is he's a nutter. Still, I can
see why he's drawn to you.

Lucy   Why?

Drinker   F.U.N.

Pause.

Fun.

Lucy   Oh, go away.

Drinker   Just look at this place. It's on its last legs. It looks ...
clapped. Enjoyed ... Enjoyed by the men of Wandsworth. Is it

still a going concern? Is it still a . . . sound business proposition, do you think? I'll tell you what; this place needs you.

Pause.

As a matter of fact, I get the feeling that if I was to proposition you right now, not in a grubby way, but in a genuine way, you'd say, 'Yes'.

Lucy   Sod off!

Drinker   Do me a favour. You're gagging for it.

She throws her drink in his face.

Lucy   Who do you think you are?

Drinker   You'd love it if I took your knickers down and stuck it right up you.

She smacks him in the face. He grabs her wrist and produces a knife. She slips the bat from under the bar and there's a stand-off.

Come on. Have a pop.

Scene Six

Bar.

Charles *enters carrying boxes of alcohol.* **Lucy** *is behind the bar, staring into space.*

Charles   Gordon's and Smirnoff thirteen to the dozen. Cunt only tried to stitch me up with more rum. Says he's got a case of Lamb's Navy written in his book. 'And I've got *cunt* written here,' I said. Lamb's Navy? What am I, a fucking sailor? I got him in the corner and I got hold of him and I said, 'Right, you cunt, right . . . Because you people do not give me the respect that I am due. Right,' I said. 'Fuck this, I'll take my business elsewhere. Fuck that,' I said. 'Because I won't take that from no one no more. Lack of respect.'

Pause.

I should have given him a slap.

Pause.

And you know me, Lucy. I'm not a violent man. What's up?

He goes through a door behind the bar to put the boxes down. He comes out.
What happened?

Lucy   He, he had a knife.

Charles   You did it again, I don't believe it.

Lucy   It happened again.

Charles   It's ridiculous!

Lucy   He attacked me.

Charles   Are you mad? My God!

Lucy *goes to him, he backs away.*

Charles   You stay away from me.

Lucy   He said I was a tart.

Charles   Well, are you?

Lucy   Don't you dare say that, what has got into you?

Charles   I'll go berserk in a minute.

Lucy   No wonder your marriage went for a Burton.

Pause.

Charles   What?

Lucy   Nothing.

Charles   What did you say?

Lucy   I'm sorry.

Charles   Who told you this?

Lucy   He did.

The **Drinker** *emerges from the back room looking stunned.*

Charles   And you believed him? Well, do you?

Lucy   No.

Charles   Well, why'd you say it?

Lucy   I don't know.

Charles   After everything I told you.

Pause.

He's a fucking boozer. Why do you talk to these people?

Lucy   He wouldn't go.

Charles   I'll make him go.

*The **Drinker** heads for the door. **Charles** follows and grabs his arm.*

Charles   Right, you cunt.

Lucy   Charles, don't.

Charles (*to **Drinker***)   What have you been saying? Eh? What did you say about me? Come on.

Drinker   What are you gonna do? Give me a slap?

Lucy   It's a wind-up. He's just trying to get a reaction.

Drinker   She told me all about you.

Charles   You should watch your fucking mouth.

Drinker   Came to me one night with such a face on her . . .

Lucy   I'm not listening.

Charles (*to **Lucy***)   No, you're all right, it's all right . . .

Charles *takes out his hankie, hands it to **Lucy**, who sniffles and blows her nose, then without looking, he turns to the **Drinker** and beats him to the floor, punching him repeatedly.*

Lucy   Stop!

Charles   You've got a reaction now!
You've got a reaction now! You've got a reaction now! Eh? Slag!

Lucy   You'll kill him!

Charles   Shut up!

*He raises his hand to slap **Lucy**.*

Lucy   No!

Charles   Get out.

Lucy   Don't you dare.

Charles   I mean it.

Lucy   I know you do, Charles.

Pause. He backs off.

Charles   It's none of your business.

Pause.

Don't look at me.

Pause.

What are you looking at?

He goes behind the bar, gets the bat. He smashes up the bar.

This? This?!

Charles *puts the bat down. Goes to the* **Drinker**. *Kneels beside him and mops blood from the* **Drinker***'s head with his shirt.*

He'll wake up in a minute. He's just drunk.
Have you got a fag?

Lucy *fetches her bag from behind the bar, rummages in it and hands him a cigarette.*

Charles   Thank you.

He puts it in his mouth and she lights it.

Thank you.

Lucy *puts a cigarette in her own mouth and lights it. The* **Drinker** *comes to and groans vaguely.*

Lucy   I never did anything, you know. Just kept them company really. Everybody's entitled to that. I don't know how I got into this mess.

Pause.

Charles   I ask myself sometimes did she step in front of the bus on purpose?

Pause.

And I tell myself that's ridiculous. I loved her. I married her.

Lucy   I couldn't do it.

Charles   I haven't got the guts.

Lucy   I've considered it.

Charles   I have too.

Lucy   Tried to think of the best way and so on.

Charles   Me too.

*The **Drinker** eyes them warily and gets up.*

Lucy   I always think of the people I'd leave behind.

Charles   Me too. That's the only thing that worries me.

Drinker   You . . . you people are mad.

Charles *pulls out his wallet and offers the **Drinker** fifty pounds.*

Charles   Go on. You're all right.

Pause.

I'm apologising.

Pause.

You don't need an extra nifty?

He adds another fifty.

A monkey?

*The **Drinker** takes the money, screws it up and tosses it in **Charles**'s face and exits.*

Charles (*snorts*)   Now I'm bribing people.

Scene Seven

Charles's flat.

Lucy and *Charles* *sit on the bed.* *Charles* *drinks from a bottle of vodka and smokes.*

Lucy   Have you ever thought about seeing a shrink?

Pause.

I mean, you were provoked, but you've been under a lot of strain. What if there's something wrong with you? I'm not saying he will press charges, but if he did . . .

Charles   'If, if, if . . . '

Lucy   Who knows what they'll find out?

Charles   If my aunty had balls she'd be my uncle.

Lucy   He'll tell them everything.

Pause.

Charles   We could go abroad. Get away from England.

Lucy   Go abroad?

Charles   Hide.

Lucy   Hide?

Charles   It's a terrible country.

Lucy   With you?

Charles   Nobody works, nobody smiles.

Lucy   I'm going home. I'm going home to watch telly and clean the cooker and do what normal people do.

Charles   I mean, I've got a conscience but I'm not going to torture myself for ever.

He picks up the Bible from by the bed, flips through it.

'The fruit of the Spirit is love, joy, peace, longsuffering, gentleness, goodness, faith, meekness and temperance.' Says who?

Pause. He drops the Bible.

Lucy   Do you believe in Heaven and Hell?

Charles   I don't know.

Lucy   I used to believe in Heaven.

Charles   I believe in Hell.

Lucy   Obviously there's a Hell.

Charles   I don't know. I don't care.

Lucy   Me neither.

Charles   Not any more.

Pause.

Lucy   I was watching telly, right, and they interviewed a man who said the anti-Christ had come and he knew who it was. He said the anti-Christ is living in south London with a woman half his age. Supposing that's true.

Pause.

Charles (*snorts*)   'The anti-Christ . . .'

Lucy   Don't laugh. I saw it on the telly.

Charles *laughs.*

Stop laughing. It makes sense to me.

Silence.

He drinks.

When my wife died, everything went with it. I didn't see the point in being good. I couldn't stop boozing, pay the bills, go to work, come home. Day after day we wade through shit.

Lucy   Oh, stop.

Charles   We grow old waiting for the big reward, something bigger than a good-night kiss, a slap on the back, a sun-tan . . .

Lucy   Now you're being silly.

Charles   The Easter Bunny, birthdays, anniversaries, 'Merry Christmas, Charles . . . Merry Christmas, everybody . . . ' I'd rather murder myself.

Lucy   That's enough of that.

Charles   She knew that this life isn't worth living. She never complained, she could always find the good in things, but deep down she knew.

Lucy   Pull yourself together.

Charles   Everybody knows, we're just taught not to think it.

Lucy   You're scaring me.

Charles   We've had it. We're doomed.

Lucy *snatches the bottle and slaps him.*

Lucy   Snap out of it, for God's sake. Do you have to go on and on and on about it? It's so selfish.

Charles   All right . . .

Lucy   It's not all right, you . . . you . . . you monster . . . what've . . . what have you done . . . ?

Pause.

Lucy *puts the bottle down and goes to the door.* **Charles** *follows.*

Charles   Where are you going?

Lucy   Home.

Charles   I'll come with you.

Lucy   Don't laugh at me.

Charles   I'm not.

Lucy   I'm not stupid.

Charles   I know.

Lucy   You don't. You think I'm just another scatty woman. It's so typical. I know you think I'm strange. People have always thought that. Even at school. 'Strange.' 'Quirky.'

'Loose.' I'm not. I'm perfectly normal. I'm just different, that's all.

Charles   I understand . . .

Lucy   Don't you dare say that. How could you understand? I hate it when people say that. People look straight through me. Like I'm invisible or a . . . a ghost or something. It drives me up the wall.

Charles *takes a step backwards and* **Lucy** *follows.*

Lucy   I'm surrounded by Evil.

Pause.

She leaves him and paces and fidgets. **Charles** *retrieves the bottle and drinks.*

Charles   I don't want you to leave because the last woman to leave me was dead within weeks.

Lucy   That's different. I don't love you.

Charles   Neither did she.

Lucy   But I like you. And . . . and . . .

Silence.

They embrace. They press their foreheads together and stay like that for a while.

Charles   Shh. It's all right.

Lucy   I'm scared.

Charles   What are you scared of?

Lucy   Everything.

Charles   Come on. I'll take you home.

Lucy   What colour are ghosts?

Charles   I don't know.

Lucy   Blue?

Charles   Shh.

Scene Eight

Church.

Charles, *wearing an old coat, sits with the* **Vicar**.

Charles   It's like there's this force controlling me or watching over me and making things happen. The things I'm afraid of, and the things I most want, they all happen but I don't ... I don't know why they happen. And, and why me anyway?

Vicar   'O Lord, thou has searched me, and known me. Thou knowest my downsitting, and mine uprising, thou understandest my thoughts from afar.'

Charles   I don't believe in God.

Vicar   Why not?

Charles   Because he doesn't understand, does he? If he did, none of this would have happened.

Pause.

Vicar   Do you believe in destiny?

Charles   I don't know what that means.

Vicar   Many people believe that events are controlled by fate which is predestined by God.

Charles   Or the Devil?

Vicar   Well, no.

Charles   Well, what are you saying?

Vicar   I'm saying perhaps it's the reason you've come to me.

Charles   I came to you because I wanted to.

Vicar   All right ...

Charles   I chose to, understand?

Vicar   Yes, yes I see.

Pause.

Charles   What about my wife? Why did that happen?

Vicar   God has called her to the kingdom of Heaven.

Charles   I know. Why?

Vicar   I don't know why.

Charles   Because it's, it's 'nice' there?

Vicar   These questions can only be answered with faith.

Charles   I don't have any faith.

Vicar   In anything?

Charles   No.

Vicar   You have no faith in humanity?

Charles   No.

Vicar   Faith in love and justice and restitution which has been with us since the birth of civilisation.

Charles   I have faith in love, yeah.

Vicar   Now we're getting somewhere.

Charles   But I don't have anyone to love.

Pause.

Vicar   Perhaps you are ready to be filled.

Charles   Filled?

Vicar   With God's love.

Charles   I don't want God's love. God's love's no good to me. Don't you understand? I've hurt people. I've done things I can't undo.

Vicar   We all hurt people.

Charles   No, I mean, really hurt people . . .

Vicar   And do you think that makes you unworthy of God's love?

Charles   Unworthy?

Vicar   Do you think that makes you unworthy of providence?

Pause.

Charles   I want to confess.

Vicar   To what?

Charles   Do it properly. 'Repent and ye shall be forgiven . . . '

Vicar   It's not that easy.

Charles   Why not?

Vicar   We do not believe in easy redemption. Your restitution is in your hands. You have to do it yourself.

Charles   I've tried doing it myself. It didn't work.

Vicar   Then I say, 'Bring forth fruits worthy of repentance.'

Charles   Listen to me . . .

Vicar   'Bring forth fruits *worthy* of repentance . . . '

Charles   Look at me . . .

Vicar   And talk to God . . .

Charles *grabs the* **Vicar** *roughly.*

Charles   I don't want to talk to God, I want to talk to you! I'm bad! All my life I've been bad! 'The brethren you deserve are manifest,' you said. What do I deserve? Eh . . . ?

He lets the **Vicar** *go.*

I'm lost. Don't you understand? I don't know who I am.

Pause.

The **Vicar** *goes.*

Scene Nine

Cemetery.

Charles, *drunk, stares at his wife's grave.*

Charles   Remember the time I tried to leave? We had a ruck in the middle of the night and I got up and got dressed but you'd hidden my shoes . . . to stop me leaving. But I went anyway . . .

in my socks. And you followed me . . . in your dressing-gown . . . and I was walking up Trinity Road and I turned around and you were all hurt and miserable and crying . . . tears streaming down your face . . . little bubbles coming out your nose . . . And you were saying, 'I just want you to come home. I just want you to come home. Don't you understand?'

Pause.

And, and I did understand.

Pause.

I just didn't know why.

Pause.

And then, despite myself, I held out my arms and you snuggled into my arms . . . and suddenly I felt warm . . . I felt part of the world again . . . it seemed like I was doing the right thing for once.

Pause.

And it was the wrong thing. And I'm sorry.

After a moment, a **Police Constable** *and a* **Woman Police Constable** *come over.* **Charles** *stands and stares at the* **WPC**.

PC   Good evening, sir.

Charles   All right?

PC   Would you like to show me some identification?

Charles   Officer, you look just like my wife.

PC   Are you going to show me some identification?

Charles   It's uncanny.

PC   Would you come with us please, sir.

Charles   This is her grave. She's dead. Completely dead.

The **WPC** *takes the bottle. The* **PC** *takes* **Charles**'s *arm.*

WPC   Would you like to go to the hospital? Is that where you're meant to be?

Charles   No. I've had a few drinks, that's all. I'll be all right in a minute . . .

He tries to walk away. They take hold of **Charles** *and pin his arms behind. He struggles.*

What are you doing?

PC   Are you going to co-operate?

Charles   I have a right to be here.

WPC   Yes, come along, don't make a fuss now.

Charles   I'm praying.

PC   I'm arresting you for threatening behaviour and drunk and disorderly conduct, understand?

Charles   I'm in mourning, the vicar knows I'm here . . . I touched his cassock, that's all, I grabbed hold of his cassock.

They pull his coat down around his arms, revealing his bloodstained shirt.

Charles   Hey, I'm not a dosser . . .

PC   What's all this?

Charles   What?

PC   This blood.

Pause.

Charles *takes out ID, gives it to the* **WPC** *who studies it and hands it to the* **PC** *who also studies it.*

Charles   Look, my name is Charles Strong. I own a bar on Garratt Lane. I've been working all night . . .

PC   Charles Strong, I'm arresting you for assault.

Charles   No, I was drunk . . . I had an accident . . .

PC   Why were you drunk?

Charles   I was a bit mixed up. Business is bad . . . one thing leads to . . .

PC   So you decided to attack somebody.

Charles No.

PC Did this person attack you?

Charles No. But ... earlier ...

PC Well, why did you attack him? Eh? You could have killed him.

Charles My wife, you see ...

PC He attacked your wife, did he?

Charles No, obviously ...

PC Obviously ... is it obvious?

Charles Listen to me, help me, please ... My wife was hit by a bus ... I had a few problems ... I was ... I was ... I was ... I was lonely ...

Pause.

And now all this ... Eh?

Pause.

PC Are you finished?

Charles It's difficult to explain.

WPC Come along then. We'll have a nice cup of tea and you can tell us all about it.

Charles You're just like her. I mean it. I think you're lovely. Isn't she lovely?

They lead him away.

Blackout.

Printed in the USA
CPSIA information can be obtained
at www.ICGtesting.com
LVHW041056171024
794057LV00001B/106